Δ The Triangle Papers: 45

An Emerging China in a World of Interdependence

A Report to
The Trilateral Commission

Authors: Yoichi Funabashi
Washington Bureau Chief
and former Beijing Correspondent,
Asahi Shimbun

Michel Oksenberg
President, East-West Center, Honolulu;
former Staff Member (China),
U. S. National Security Council

Heinrich Weiss
Chairman of the Managing Board, SMS AG,
Düsseldorf; Chairman, China Committee,
East Committee of German Industry

published by
The Trilateral Commission
New York, Paris and Tokyo
May 1994

Library of Congress Cataloging-in-Publication Data

Funabashi, Yoichi, 1944-
An Emerging China in a World of Interdependence: a report to the
    Trilateral Commission/authors, Yoichi Funabashi, Michel
    Oksenberg, Heinrich Weiss.

    p. cm. — (The Triangle papers: 45)
Includes bibliographical references.
ISBN 0-930503-71-6: $12.00
1. China—Relations—Foreign countries. 2. China—Economic
policy—1976- 3. China—Politics and government—1976-
I. Oksenberg, Michel, 1938- . II. Weiss, Heinrich. III. Title. IV. Series.
DS740.4.F8 1994
951.05—dc20

                                                            94-16060
                                                               CIP
Manufactured in the United States of America

THE TRILATERAL COMMISSION

345 East 46th Street	c/o Japan Center for	35, avenue de Friedland
New York, NY 10017	International Exchange	75008 Paris, France
	4-9-17 Minami-Azabu	
	Minato-ku	
	Tokyo, Japan	

The Authors

YOICHI FUNABASHI is a diplomatic correspondent and columnist for the *Asahi Shimbun*, a leading Japanese daily. Since September 1993 he has been the *Asahi* Bureau Chief in Washington, D.C. He served earlier as an *Asahi* correspondent in Beijing. Dr. Funabashi was a Nieman Fellow at Harvard University in 1976-77, an Ushiba Fellow in 1986, and a Fellow at the Institute for International Economics (Washington, D.C.) in 1987. He is the author of several books, including *The Theory of Economic Security* (1978), *Naibu—Inside China* (1983), *The U.S.-Japan Economic Entanglement: The Inside Story* (1987) and *Nihon Senryaku Sengen* [Civilian Manifesto] (1991, editor and author). Winner of the Suntory Humanities Award in 1983, he was also awarded the Vaughn-Ueda Prize—often called Japan's Pulitzer Prize—in 1985 for his coverage of U.S.-Japan economic friction, the Yoshino Sakuzo Award in 1988 for his book *Managing the Dollar: From the Plaza to the Louvre,* and the Ishibashi Tanzan Prize in 1992 for his articles "Japan and the New World Order" for *Foreign Affairs* and "Japan and America: Global Partnership" for *Foreign Policy.*

MICHEL OKSENBERG is President of the East-West Center in Honolulu, Hawaii. He was previously Professor of Political Science and Director of the Center for Chinese Studies at the University of Michigan. His teaching and writing focus on Chinese domestic affairs, Chinese foreign policy, and Sino-American relations. Educated at Swarthmore College (B.A., 1960) and Columbia University (Ph.D., 1969), he was Assistant Professor at Stanford University (1966-68) and Assistant and Associate Professor at Columbia University (1968-74) before joining the University of Michigan faculty in 1973. From 1977 to 1980, he served as a staff member of the U. S. National Security Council with special responsibility for China and the Indochina states. In 1987, he became China advisor to the Washington law firm of Akin, Gump, Strauss, Hauer, and Feld. Dr. Oksenberg is a frequent contributor to journals such as *The China Quarterly* (serving on the editorial board), *Problems of Communism, Asian Survey,* and *Foreign Affairs.* His recent books include *Policy Making in China: Leaders, Structure, and Processes* (1988, co-author); *China's Participation in the IMF, the World Bank, and GATT: Toward a Global Economic Order* (1990, co-author); and *Beijing Spring, 1989: Confrontation and Conflict* (1990, co-editor).

HEINRICH WEISS is Chairman of the Managing Board and shareholder of SMS Aktiengesellschaft, based in Düsseldorf, the holding firm of a group of companies active worldwide (including in China for over three decades) in designing and manufacturing machinery and complete plants for steel, aluminum and plastic processing. He is also Chairman of the China Committee in the East Committee of German Industry, based in Cologne. Educated in electrical engineering at Munich University, he began his career in 1971 as President, Chief Executive Officer and shareholder of Siemag Siegener Maschinenbau, based in Hilchenbach. After the merger with Schloemann AG, a competitor, in 1974, he assumed his present position as Chairman of the SMS Schloemann-Siemag group. He is also a director of various banks and industrial companies. Mr. Weiss has served as Chairman of the Federation of German Industries (BDI), in 1991-92. He was also Chairman of the economic advisory council of the CDU Party in 1983-88.

The Trilateral Process

The report which follows is the joint responsibility of the three authors, with Yoichi Funabashi serving as the lead author. Although only the authors are responsible for the analysis and conclusions, they have been aided in the work by many others. The authors would like to express particular appreciation to Charles Morrison, Director of the International Program on Economics and Politics at the East-West Center in Honolulu, who has been helpful in discussions and with drafting suggestions throughout the project. The three Directors of the Trilateral Commission—Tadashi Yamamoto, Charles Heck, and Paul Révay—provided critical help in the preparation of this report, each in his own way. The authors also particularly appreciate the help provided by Louise Price of the *Asahi Shimbun* Washington staff, by Makito Noda of the Japanese Trilateral staff, and by Monika Lützow, Manager of the China Committee in the East Committee of German Industry.

The generous financial support provided by the Henry Luce Foundation is greatly appreciated.

Thinking about this project began in 1992 and it was launched in early 1993. A first outline for the report was provided by Yoichi Funabashi to his co-authors in June 1993. The first authors' meeting was in Honolulu on August 1, including Funabashi, Oksenberg, Yamamoto, and Morrison. Weiss provided written input from the European side. The main thrusts of the report were discussed at this meeting, and a second outline developed. Funabashi discussed the project with Japanese Trilateral members and experts in Tokyo on August 26. Weiss discussed the project with European Trilateral members (and a few Japanese and North Americans) at the time of the European Group's fall meeting in Barcelona, on October 15.

The second authors' meeting was in New York City on November 10. Funabashi provided the basis for discussion with sketches of most chapters. Part of this day was spent in discussion with several Chinese experts. In January 1994, Heinrich Weiss discussed the report in London, Paris, Brussels and Bonn—in meetings including Trilateral members and relevant officials and experts. On February 17 and 18 in New York City and Washington, D.C., Oksenberg and Funabashi met with U.S. and Canadian Trilateral members, officials and experts.

The third authors' meeting was in Washington on February 19-20. Discussion focussed on the first draft of the report prepared by

Funabashi. Key themes in the report were discussed with a number of Chinese experts on February 20.

The second draft of the report, completed in late March, was discussed at the 1994 annual meeting of the Trilateral Commission, in Tokyo on April 9-11. The annual meeting also included a session led by three Chinese experts. A discussion of the draft report with Japanese experts took place on April 8, just before the annual meeting. The third and final draft of the report was completed later in April.

The persons consulted spoke for themselves as individuals and not as representatives of any institutions with which they are associated. Those consulted or otherwise assisting in the development of the report included:

Michel Albert, *Member of the Monetary Policy Council of the Banque de France; former Chairman, Assurances Générales de France; former High Commissioner of the French Planning Agency*

Jacques Andrieu, *Director of Research (China), French National Centre for Scientific Research (CNRS)*

Claude Aubert, *Director of Research, French National Institute for Agronomic Research (INRA)*

Georges Berthoin, *International Honorary Chairman, European Movement; Honorary European Chairman, The Trilateral Commission, Paris*

John Beyer, *Director, China-Britain Trade Group, London*

Claude Blanchemaison, *Director for Asia, French Ministry of Foreign Affairs*

Jean Bonvin, *President, OECD Development Center, Paris*

Pierre Callebaut, *Chairman, Amylum, Brussels; former Chairman, Belgian Federation of Agricultural and Food Industries*

Hervé de Carmoy, *Chairman, Banque Industrielle Mobilière et Privée (B.I.M.P.); former Chief Executive, Société Générale de Belgique, Brussels*

Joseph Caron, *Director, North Asia Relations Division, Department of Foreign Affairs (Canada)*

Frédéric de Castro, *Secretary, French Group of Trilateral Commission; Financial Director, Rexel, Paris*

Chen Qimao, *Chairman, Academic Advisory Council, Shanghai Institute for International Studies*

André Chieng, *Chairman, Asiatique Européenne de Commerce, Paris*

Dominique Clavel, *Senior Vice President, Chase Manhattan Bank*

Alain Cotta, *Professor of Economics and Management, University of Paris*

Gerald L. Curtis, *Professor of Political Science, East Asian Institute, Columbia University*

Dominik Declercq, *Brussels*

Baron Guido Declercq, *Chairman, Fidisco, Investvo and Benevent, Brussels; Honorary General Administrator, Kath University, Leuven*

Jean Deflassieux, *Chairman, Banque des Echanges Internationaux; Honorary Chairman, Crédit Lyonnais, Paris*

Ding Jingping, *Deputy Director, Institute of Industrial Economics, Chinese Academy of Social Sciences, Beijing*

Sir Alan Donald, *Former British Ambassador to China*

Erin Endean, *Director, Hills & Company; former Director of Chinese and Japanese Affairs, Office of U.S. Trade Representative*

Victor Falkenheim, *Department of Political Science, University of Toronto*

Peter Ferdinand, *Royal Institute for International Affairs, London; Warwick University*

Charles Freeman, *Assistant Secretary for Regional Security Affairs, U.S. Department of Defense*

Orit Frenkel, *Senior Manager, International Trade/Investment, General Electric*

Kiichiro Fukasaku, *OECD Development Centre, Paris*

Shinji Fukukawa, *Executive Vice President, Kobe Steel Co. Ltd.*

Jeffrey Garten, *Under Secretary for International Trade, U.S. Department of Commerce*

John Gilbert, *Member of British Parliament (Labour); former Treasury, Transport and Defense Minister; Chairman of John Gilbert & Associates*

François Godement, *Senior Research Associate on China/Asia, French Institute for International Relations (IFRI); Professor, National Institute of Oriental Languages & Civilizations (INALCO), Paris*

Baron Jacques Groothaert, *Honorary Chairman of the Board, Générale de Banque, Brussels; former Ambassador of Belgium to China*

Earl of Harrowby, *Chairman, The Private Bank, London*

Ruth Hayhoe, *Ontario Institute for Studies in Education*

Charles Heck, *North American Director, Trilateral Commission*

Peter Howell, *Group Marketing Executive, Asia Pacific, Citibank*

Christopher Hum, *Assistant Under-Secretary of State (Northern Asia), Foreign and Commonwealth Office, London*

Sir Michael Jenkins, *Executive Director, Kleinwort Benson Ltd., London*

Ji Guoxing, *Director of Asian Pacific Studies, Shanghai Institute for International Studies*

Jin Dexiang, *Vice President, China Institute of Contemporary International Relations (CICIR), Beijing*

Alain Joly, *Member of the Board and Managing Director, L'Air Liquide, Paris*

Beryl Joncour-Chapuis, *Vice-President, Alcatel CIT, Paris*

Karl Kaiser, *Director, Research Institute of German Society for Foreign Affairs, Bonn; Professor of International Relations, Bonn University*

Hiroshi Peter Kamura, *Trilateral Commission (Japan); Executive Director, Japan Center for International Exchange, U.S.A.*

Ryosei Kokubun, *Professor of Chinese Politics, Keio University*

Michael Kramer, *Chief Political Correspondent,* Time

Horst Krenzler, *Director General for External Relations, European Commission, Brussels*

Count Otto Lambsdorff, *Member of German Bundestag; President, Liberal International; Honorary Chairman, Free Democratic Party; former Federal Minister of Economics*

David Michael Lampton, *President, National Committee on U.S.-China Relations, New York City*

Alan Lee Williams, *Director, British Atlantic Council, London*

Pierre Lellouche, *Member of National Assembly and Defense Spokesman for the RPR, Paris*

Li Luye, *Director-General, China Center for International Studies (CCIS), Beijing; former Chinese Ambassador to the United Nations*

James Lilley, *Former U. S. Ambassador to the People's Republic of China*

Winston Lord, *U.S. Assistant Secretary of State for East Asian and Pacific Affairs*

Monika Lützow, *Manager of the China Group, East Committee of German Industry, Cologne*

Jean-Louis Martin, *Economist (China/Asia Dept.), Banque Indosuez, Paris*

Gilles Martinet, *Ambassadeur de France; President, Association for the European Cultural Community, Paris*

Count Albrecht Matuschka, *Chairman, Matuschka Group, Munich*

Hanns Maull, *Professor of International Relations, University of Trier*

Laure Mellerio, *General Secretary, France-China Committee, Paris*

Charles Morrison, *Director, International Program on Economics and Politics, East-West Center, Honolulu*

Masashi Nishihara, *Director, First Research Department, National Institute for Defense Studies; Professor of International Relations, National Defense Academy*

Makito Noda, *Trilateral Commission (Japan); Senior Program Officer, Japan Center for International Exchange, Tokyo*

Shijuro Ogata, *Advisor, Yamaichi Securities, Co. Ltd.*

Hisashi Owada, *Japanese Ambassador to the United Nations; former Vice Minister of Foreign Affairs*

Sir Michael Palliser, *Vice Chairman, Samuel Montagu & Co.; former Permanent Under-Secretary of State, Foreign and Commonwealth Office, London; President, China-Britain Trade Group*

Pan Zhenqiang, *Director, Institute for Strategic Studies, National Defense University, Beijing*

G. Martin Prada, *China Desk (DG1), European Commission, Brussels*

Louise Price, Asahi Shimbun, *Washington Bureau*

Paul Révay, *European Director, Trilateral Commission*

Rozanne Ridgway, *Co-Chair, Atlantic Council; former U.S. Assistant Secretary of State for European and Canadian Affairs*

Lord Rippon of Hexham, *Chairman, Unichem and Dun & Bradstreet, London; former British Cabinet Minister*

David Rockefeller, *Founder and Honorary Chairman, Trilateral Commission*

John Roper, *Director, Institute for Security Studies, Western European Union; former Member of British Parliament*

François de Rose, *Ambassadeur de France; former Permanent Representative to NATO*

Kiichi Saeki, *Deputy Chairman, International Institute for Global Peace*

Gerald Segal, *International Institute for Strategic Studies, London; Editor,* The Pacific Review

Masahide Shibusawa, *Director, East-West Seminar, Tokyo*

Peter Shore, *Member of British Parliament (Labour)*

Dan Snyder, *Assistant to the President, East-West Center, Honolulu*

Paula Stern, *Senior Fellow, Progressive Policy Institute, Washington, D.C.; former Chairwoman, U.S. International Trade Commission*

Nick Swales, *Executive Assistant, Canadian Group of the Trilateral Commission*

Sir Peter Tapsell, *Member of British Parliament (Conservative)*

Jacques Thierry, *Chairman of the Board, Banque Bruxelles Lambert; Chairman of the Board, Artois Piedboeuf Interbrew, Brussels*

Ko-Yung Tung, *Chairman, Global Practice Group, O'Melveny & Myers, New York City*

Ernesto Vellano, *Secretary of the Italian Group, Trilateral Commission; International Consultant, Rome*

François de Villepin, *Chairman, France-China Committee, Paris*

Ezra Vogel, *U.S. Central Intelligence Agency*

Angelika Volle, *Secretary Treasurer of the German Group, Trilateral Commission; Chief Editor,* Europa Archiv, *Bonn*

Mary Wadsworth-Darby, *Executive Director, America-China Society*

Wan Guang, *Senior Research Fellow and Member of the Executive Board, China Center for International Studies (CCIS), Beijing; Professor, Department of International Politics, People's University of China*

Serge Weinberg, *Chairman and Chief Executive Officer, Rexel; Member of the Board and Director General, Pinault Group, Paris*

Norbert Wieczorek, *Member of the German Bundestag and Spokesperson on International Economic and Monetary Affairs of the SPD Parliamentary Group*

Lord Wilson of Tillyorn, *Former Governor of Hong Kong* (1987-1992)

Peter Witte, *Assistant to the North American Director, Trilateral Commission*

Otto Wolff von Amerongen, *Chairman, East Committee of the German Industry; Chairman and Chief Executive Officer, Otto Wolff Industrieberatung und Beteiligung, Cologne*

Xu Jian, *Researcher, China Center for International Studies (CCIS), Beijing*

Tadashi Yamamoto, *Japanese Director, Trilateral Commission; President, Japan Center for International Exchange*

Takaaki Yokota, *Professor, Chubu University*

Yuan Ming, *Director, Institute of International Relations, Peking University*

Bernhard Zepter, *Cabinet of the President of the European Commission (International Affairs), Brussels*

Zhan Shiliang, *Deputy Director-General, China Center for International Studies (CCIS), Beijing; former Ambassador to Egypt and Turkey*

Zhou Xiaochuan, *Executive Vice President, Bank of China*

Table of Contents

I. INTRODUCTION:
A NEW RISING POWER

Over the past century, the rise of new powers has posed great challenges and opportunities for the established world order. Thus, the rise of the United States, Germany, and Japan in the late 1800s and early 1900s necessitated massive adjustments to the international system led by Britain and France. The rise of the Soviet Union disrupted the aspirations for a harmonious post-World War II order led by the United States. The postwar rise of Japan and the European Community strained international monetary and trading arrangements (and encouraged creation of the Trilateral Commission, among other responses).

Now, the world—and particularly the Trilateral countries—faces the prospect of a new rapidly rising power: China. Its rise is propelled by its robust economic performance. With considerable unevenness and starting from a low base, its economy has been expanding at an average annual rate of 7-8 percent for nearly 40 years; and in the past ten years the pace has dramatically accelerated. The increased economic weight of China is most sharply portrayed using purchasing-power-parity (PPP) exchange rates, as in the IMF's revised weights for its *World Economic Outlook*.[1] Using the traditional measure of current exchange rates, the Chinese economy's share in the world economy hardly changed from 1970 to 1990, hovering around 2 percent (the smallest of the G-7 economies, Canada, was at 2.58 percent on this scale in 1990). Using a PPP-based measure, the weight of the Chinese economy rose from somewhat under 3 percent in 1970 to over 6 percent in 1990—not far behind Japan at 7.63 percent and well above all other G-7 economies except the United States. While most of China's 1.2 billion people still rank among the lower third or half of the world's population in terms of per capita income and consumption, the People's Republic of China is reaching the top ranks of many indicators of aggregate economic size. China is now among the ten largest exporting countries. Energy consumption in China is exceeded only by the United States.[2]

China's rise offers the Trilateral countries not only major economic opportunities, but basic political and security opportunities as well.

Twenty years ago, many people believed that North-South tensions—the rivalries between the developed and developing countries—would be the major source of global instability in the 21st century. These people believed that Cold War tensions between the Soviet bloc and the Trilateral countries would eventually be surmounted (though few predicted the collapse of the Soviet Union). They believed North-South tensions were more enduring, pervasive, and unremediable. The development of China is removing a substantial portion of humankind from the ranks of the poor, further blurring the distinction between developed and developing countries. The challenges which China's rise presents are far more welcome than the problems that would have existed if China had remained unambiguously among the ranks of the poor and underdeveloped.

A sense of realism is necessary, however, to grasp the opportunities and challenges that China's rise presents. Four factors particularly merit attention:

- First, China's trajectory to date suggests it will emerge as a *complete* power. That is, as its officials acknowledge, its leaders wish their nation to be wealthy and powerful. In contrast to the Soviet Union, which had military power without economic strength, or Japan, which is economically powerful but militarily constrained, China is likely to emerge as a "comprehensive power," with both economic and military strength. Its accrual of power will be protracted, but no one should doubt the determination of China's leaders—either today or in the future—to have a prominent and respected voice in shaping the world's and their region's destiny, and to acquire the weaponry that they believe will give added credibility to their voice.

- Second, China's rise coincides with the globalization of manufacturing processes, the telecommunications transformation, and the internationalization of financial markets. The possibility exists of weaving China into an interdependent world at a relatively early stage in its rise, thereby increasing its stake in a stable world order. It is also a matter of urgency to involve China in addressing a range of issues that endanger the welfare of all humankind, such as global climatic change, environmental degradation, loss of bio-diversity, dissemination of weapons of mass destruction, and historically unprecedented increases in population. No adequate response to these issues is conceivable without China's active cooperation.

- Third, China challenges traditional concepts about rising powers. In the past, rising states have controlled their boundaries, had minimal social unrest, and had settled institutional arrangements. China's rise, however, is occurring under conditions of uncertainty. Many fundamental constitutional issues confront the Chinese polity: the distribution of authority between the center and the provinces, civil-military arrangements, the procedures for orderly succession and transfer of power from one ruler to the next, the role of the ruling Communist Party, and the role of representative assemblies and parliaments. Further, the mainland government, although recognized by most countries as the legitimate government of China, is not the only entity of Chinese ethnicity. Three ethnic Chinese entities—Taiwan, Hong Kong, and mainland China—form an increasingly intertwined economic zone. Similar trans-state economic zones are linking portions of China with Thailand and Burma in the southwest, with the Central Asian republics in the northwest, and with Russia, North and South Korea, and Japan in the northeast. Even as mainland China rises, its control over the flow of goods, ideas, and people across its border is eroding. Hence, China in the years ahead is likely to be territorially amorphous, economically dynamic, culturally proud, socially unstable, and politically unsettled. These qualities have not co-existed in previous rising powers, and they will require a distinctive set of responses.

- Fourth, China's rise is occurring while the energies of the established powers are consumed by domestic political and economic concerns and while their leaders are particularly weak. To the extent the Trilateral countries attach priority to foreign affairs, their attention is focused elsewhere. The attention that China receives tends to be sporadic, and the signals emitted tend to be inconsistent. High-level dialogue with China's leaders cultivated in the 1970s—by persons such as Henry Kissinger, Zbigniew Brzezinski, Edward Heath, Franz-Josef Strauss, and several Japanese—was not sustained in the 1980s. Opportunities have been neglected to share and shape perspectives on the nature of the post-Cold War era and to nurture the sense of responsibility that should accompany great-power status. As a result, China's cooperation must be elicited on headline-grabbing transitory issues—such as the Iraqi invasion of Kuwait, North Korea's acquisition of nuclear weapons, or Beijing's treatment of specific dissidents—without a shared conceptual framework having been established to illuminate for the Chinese why it is in their interest to resolve the problem at hand. The established powers therefore find themselves as the *demandeur* of the rising power, giving China leverage, when the process should entail mutual accommodation.

This report charts a course for the Trilateral countries in dealing with China. It considers China's rise more an opportunity than a threat, and recommends a wide range of economic, strategic, and political actions that would facilitate China's involvement in the world community. At the same time, it recommends that expectations be kept realistic. All too often, China's partners have harbored unrealistic hopes for China, and when unmet, China has been blamed for dashing the unrealistic dreams of others. China, after all, is a great civilization, with its own history and traditions. Its path will be shaped largely by internal forces and the choices of its leaders. As the outside world seeks to incorporate China in the emerging world order, it must be remembered that China's leaders will wish to shape that order to suit their interests and to govern their country in accord with their own vision. The process of meeting this challenge will be a protracted one, involving decades and generations, marked by moments of great triumph and severe setbacks. Patience and persistence are requisites for staying the course.

The interests of the Trilateral countries toward China obviously differ and preclude pursuit of a totally coordinated policy. As distant powers, without alliance obligations, the continental Western Europeans do not bear responsibilities for maintaining a stable balance of power in the region. Britain has obligations toward Hong Kong, and the United States has legislation governing its relations with Taiwan. Japan has a historical involvement with China that neither Europe nor North America shares, while the United States has long exhibited a missionary and ideological zeal toward China that neither Japan nor Europe shares.

Despite these differences, a major set of interests is shared. These can be grouped into several categories or "baskets": (1) international strategic interests, where the Trilateral countries seek cooperative, responsible behavior by China as a permanent member of the United Nations Security Council, unambiguous Chinese adherence to the Nuclear Non-Proliferation Treaty and the Missile Technology Control Regime, conventional weapons sales policies that do not disturb regional balances, and acceptance of existing limits on nuclear testing; (2) regional security interests, such as assistance in maintenance of stability on the Korean peninsula and in Indochina and resolution of conflicting territorial claims in the East and South China Seas; (3) interests in Beijing's adherence to the agreements reached with the United Kingdom concerning Hong Kong's governance after 1997 and in the continued ability of the people of Taiwan to enjoy a tranquil, prosperous future under increasingly democratic rule; (4) in accord with the United Nations Universal Declaration of Human Rights, interests in the Chinese government's protection of the basic human rights of its people, out of recognition that any government's failure to adhere to this standard adversely affects the welfare of all humanity; (5) economic interests in facilitating China's sustainable growth, in securing market access, and in obtaining a continued orderly Chinese entry into world markets; and (6) interests in obtaining China's cooperation in addressing the problems of interdependence mentioned above (environmental degradation, population migration, and so on). And for China to be able to respond to these interests, the Trilateral countries have an even more fundamental interest: its effective and good governance, which requires a unified, modernizing, stable, and humanely governed China.

Clearly, the Trilateral countries have a substantial number of significant interests at stake with China. Most of these interests, it should be noted, correspond with the interests of China's leaders to develop their country in a tranquil environment. Even with the overlap, however, the Trilateral countries seek to influence Chinese behavior on a wider range of issues than they have the capacity to affect over the short run. This necessitates having a sense of priorities and a strategy for encouraging the desired Chinese responses. The priorities recommended in this report are in the security and economic domains and in assisting development of institutions contributing to China's effective and good governance. Each of the baskets is important, however, and the Trilateral countries should maintain loose linkages among them. That is, progress on all the issues should be quietly reviewed during regular, high-level meetings, and the Chinese leaders must come to understand that failure to advance in one area will restrain progress in other areas. But preconditions should be avoided, i.e., explicitly demanding progress in one area in order to advance another.

This strategy entails approaching China from positions of strength, weaving China into webs of economic interdependence, engaging China in the global economy and in multilateral security arrangements, maintaining frequent extensive high-level dialogue with Chinese leaders, and recognizing the important roles that NGOs and the private sector must play in integrating China with the world community. The positions of strength include a forward-deployed American military presence, vibrant Japanese-American and Korean-American alliances, the continued prosperity and stability of Taiwan and the ASEAN states (with that development extending to Vietnam, Laos, Cambodia, and Burma), and the development of regional and sub-regional organizations and processes in which China is involved.

The following eight chapters elaborate on the themes mentioned above:

Chapter II: China in Historical Perspective
To understand China today and the challenges that lie ahead, one must appreciate the country's culture and history. It is necessary to be sensitive to both the pride of most Chinese in their ancient civilization and their fears from its more recent traumatic past under foreign domination. A better understanding of both elements in the Chinese psyche can be a great help in guiding Trilateral policy.

Chapter III: The Mainland Domestic Context
Accurately assessing China's current condition—politically, economically, militarily—is fundamental to understanding its future. Outlining the certainties (such as the continuation of economic reform) and the uncertainties (such as the outcome of the leadership transition) helps set the stage for further discussion of China as it is and will be.

Chapter IV: Hong Kong, Taiwan, and "Greater China"
China's division into three parts—mainland China, Hong Kong and Taiwan—greatly complicates international integrative efforts. Some see the emergence of a "Greater China," but this notion is of limited utility.

Chapter V: The Chinese Economy: Regional and Global Dimensions
This chapter will delve more deeply into the policy issues associated with China's economic growth and entry into the international economy. Trilateral countries face policy issues in several areas: Chinese exports, China's import strategy, technology transfer to China, direct investment, and most-favored-nation (MFN) status with the United States. Ways of integrating China with regional and world organizations such as APEC and GATT will also be explored.

Chapter VI: China's National Security
This chapter examines the military and security dimensions of China's emergence as a great power. What are China's security needs and aspirations? How will China's growing role as an arms supplier affect the international order? What positive contributions might China make in reshaping the regional and global order in the post-Cold War era? The policy implications for the Trilateral countries of a "security partnership" with China are also addressed.

Chapter VII: Global Issues and China's Role
Health and population issues, environmental degradation, and non-proliferation are some of the concerns addressed in this chapter.

Chapter VIII: The Effective and Good Governance of China
After a discussion of how Chinese think about the task of governance, this chapter examines the implications for political reform of economic development and of China's recent traumatic history. How should the interest of the Trilateral countries in the effective and good governance of China be expressed?

Chapter IX: Summary of Policy Recommendations
This concluding chapter will summarize and draw together our recommendations to Trilateral countries.

II. China in Historical Perspective

China's past is an essential part of its present. From peasants in remote rural villages to today's rulers still ensconced in the splendors of Beijing's Imperial Palace, Chinese are rooted in their ancient civilization. Most know the history of their families stretching back for several if not dozens of generations. They learned about the great battles fought near their villages a generation or a millennium ago and the biographies of famous officials who hailed from their counties in previous dynasties. While the bonds linking ordinary Chinese to their nation's past have atrophied under Communist rule, memories of distant and recent history deeply color the approach of China's leaders and their populace at large to the governance of their country and to foreign affairs.

THE BURDEN OF GREATNESS

Etched in most Chinese minds is the continuity of the civilization and the glory of its accomplishments in the Han, Tang, Ming, and Qing dynasties. China has achieved greatness when it has been unified and ordered its realm. Weakness, brought on by internal misrule, invited foreign aggression, civil war, and domestic calamity.

Since time immemorial, Chinese leaders have instructed intellectuals to write history not for accuracy but to make moral judgments and draw lessons for the present. Hence, Chinese history honors those who unified China and made it wealthy and powerful. It dishonors those who contributed to its fragmentation, undermined its ethic, and facilitated its conquest by foreigners.

The burden this historiography places on China's rulers is enormous. Their duty is to restore the nation's greatness, to protect its unity and prevent its humiliation. They know future historians will judge them by this exacting standard.

But Chinese are also misguided by the historiography. In at least four important ways, as the eminent Harvard Sinologist John Fairbank noted in the magisterial history he completed just before his death, the Chinese awareness of their own past is as much myth as reality.[1] First, the outside world—especially Indian and Tibetan civilization through Buddhism and Inner Asian cultures through the incursions of Turkic, Mongol, and other peoples from the Asian heartland—had a tremendous impact upon the evolution of Chinese civilization. Thus, Chinese culture today is not simply a lineal descendent of the Han people who settled the Yellow River basin and spread from there, as the national myth would have it. It is an amalgam of the powerful Han culture (and the many indigenous civilizations which the Han absorbed as they spread across China) and the foreign civilizations which swept across China and over the Han.

Second, the myth that helped sustain imperial rule was of an East Asian order in which rulers on the periphery acknowledged the moral superiority of the emperor and paid deference to him through periodic ritual visits to the Forbidden City in Beijing.[2] According to the myth, the political dominance of the emperor and his bureaucracy brought tranquillity to this Asian world. Recent scholarship challenges the accuracy of the image. The deference that many rulers exhibited was more symbolic than real. Relations between the Ming (1368-1644) and Qing (1644-1911) courts and Korea and Japan were much more complicated than the myth would have it, and the same was true for much of Southeast and Inner Asia. The emperor's main concern was not to have overt challenges to the myth, since his real need was to use ritualistic external deference to enhance his domestic legitimacy. Most rulers on the periphery were prepared to indulge the emperor as long as he did not interfere in their internal affairs and came to their assistance if they faced unmanageable opposition. When a state refused to conform to the emperor's ritualistic needs, he was prepared to deal with the idiosyncratic interests of the claimant, as with the Russians in the 1600s and the British in Nepal in the 1700s. But the subtleties of the traditional system and the operating constraints on Chinese imperial power tended to be conveniently neglected in Chinese historiography, so that in today's world, what is erroneously recalled both in China and among its neighbors is a traditional East Asian order dominated by China. And China's neighbors wonder whether China's future leaders will seek to recreate a modern version of this perceived past. Beijing's leaders harbor their own images of China's role at moments of national greatness. These find expression in some of the rituals involved in a state visit to Beijing or in the combination of arrogance and benevolence China exhibits toward weaker neighbors.

Third, traditional historiography portrays the polity as having been dominated and unified by the Mandarinate class of bureaucrats, landed gentry, and intellectuals in service to the emperor. This ruling elite unified the realm in large measure through its commitment to and propagation of Confucianism, the state ideology. Commerce and merchants were supposedly subordinate to bureaucracy and the Mandarins. Recent scholarship on China portrays a much more complex picture of the traditional and evolving political and social systems.[3] Merchants and artisans were politically more influential than the myth allowed.

And fourth, the image of the Chinese world order was that commerce with the outside world was confined to officially sanctioned trade which occurred at officially designated spots on the periphery or which accompanied missions of "barbarians" paying tribute to the emperor. Recent scholarly research reveals that considerable unreported commerce—often labeled "piracy"—occurred with the connivance of local officials, especially along the coast.

These four distortions that Chinese have perpetuated about their history—exaggerating imperial dominance of the Asian order, neglecting the role of the outside world, denigrating the importance of commerce and merchants, and minimizing the trade and entrepreneurship that existed along the coast—were crucial in promoting imperial, bureaucratic rule and facilitating the unity of the country. But these misperceptions about the past have become part of popular Trilateral conceptions about China as well. And they must be seen as misperceptions in order to understand the present. This is not to say that there was no truth in the myths. Chinese civilization does exhibit remarkable continuities from its neolithic past to the present. China did not confront a serious external rival from the 1400s until the arrival of the British in the 1800s. The bureaucratic class did enjoy preeminence over the merchants. And foreign trade was constrained. But the opening to the outside world, the ability to deal with independent states as equals, the unleashing of entrepreneurial talents, and the expansion of foreign trade are not totally alien to the Chinese experience. Indigenous traditions, particularly along the China coast, exist in support of the policy directions of the Deng era.[4]

CHINA'S EXPERIENCE WITH TRILATERAL COUNTRIES

No less complicated was China's experience with the Trilateral countries from the 1840s to 1949.[5] Most Chinese associate the West and Japan with aggression and exploitation. The period from the Opium War to the Communist takeover is termed a century of humiliation, and in no small measure, the Communist Party had as its initial purpose the total ending of foreign privileges. Thus, Mao Zedong proclaimed, when founding the People's Republic on October 1, 1949, "The Chinese people have stood up. They will never again be humiliated."

Not everything the West and Japan did in China was unremittingly bleak and destructive. To be sure, the Japanese invasion was brutal and Chinese suffered many indignities under Western rule in the Treaty Ports. But the West and Japan left positive legacies and some fond memories as well. The imperialist system in China stimulated some (while disrupting other) portions of the evolving traditional economy. China's leading universities and hospitals were, for the most part, established by foreign missionaries, foundations, and governments. Westerners helped create modern newspapers and trained journalists to staff them. Japan, Germany, France, Britain and the United States shaped efforts in the first half of this century to draft various civil and criminal legal codes. Western banks helped create the foundations of a modern banking system. Many Chinese students who studied in Japan, Europe, and North America contributed to the development of their country. Various academic disciplines—ranging from chemistry to economics to sociology and social work—were established in Chinese universities, their faculty drawn from Chinese who had been trained abroad. And a wide range of concepts previously not well-developed in the Chinese philosophical lexicon—pragmatism, human rights, liberty, socialism, individualism—began to circulate among and stimulate Chinese intellectuals.

All this, of course, was disruptive to the traditional system, which in any case was in decay and difficulty before the Western and Japanese onslaught. Even as the West undermined the traditional system, however, the outside world also offered competing solutions to the Chinese situation: Christianity, liberalism, democracy, federalism, fascism, communism. And it educated many Chinese who understood and accepted some of these previously alien notions and integrated them with their own indigenous beliefs. Out of this complex encounter with the outside world grew the four underlying questions with which Chinese leaders and intellectuals have grappled as they sought a Chinese path to modernity: What to accept from the West in order to meet its challenge? What to retain from the Chinese past in order to preserve the essence of the civilization? What to reject from the West because it would erode the Chinese essence? And what of the past to jettison because it would prevent the modernization of China? These four questions have been at the heart of the political debates in China, and various responses to them have defined the Chinese political spectrum for over a century.

The legacy of China's experience with imperialism is complicated. Though some Chinese are deeply anti-Western and others are totally admiring, most are deeply ambivalent. On the one hand, there is continued bitterness and mistrust. Behavior that affronts Chinese dignity, intrudes on the Chinese sense of sovereignty, or threatens exploitation draws a quick rebuff. But on the other hand, there is appreciation of what the West offers, not just in the realm of science and technology but, to those Chinese who have had a sustained and not humiliating exposure to the West, an appreciation of its culture and values as well.

In sum, the Trilateral countries left dual legacies in China. The West helped create an intense nationalism that can become irrational and dangerous when fed by the provincialism and xenophobia of the hinterland. But the West also created an internationalism, a desire to be part of the world community, to meet international standards, and to contribute to humankind as an equal. In the 1950s and 1960s, led by the United States, the Trilateral countries helped provoke the anti-Western, provincial and xenophobic face of China. In the 1970s and 1980s, the Trilateral countries built upon their more positive legacies and helped to elicit the sophisticated international face of China. The challenge of the 1990s and beyond is to sustain that effort under possibly more trying circumstances.

III. THE MAINLAND DOMESTIC CONTEXT

Several insights about mainland China should be kept in mind as one assesses the current scene. China is a land of contrast and paradox. The country is so vast and varied that almost any observation about it is true, but the opposite is also true. Further, the Chinese condition is never as good as it appears at its best moments, and never as bad as it appears in its worst moments. Superficially, China appears to be constantly changing, but underneath the surface, there is considerable continuity in beliefs, institutions and behavior.

Moreover, uncertainty is a permanent condition of modern China. For over a century, unexpected, major developments have taken both Chinese and the outside world by surprise. China's developmental path has been a tortuous one. Periods of upheaval and turmoil—the Boxer rebellion, the Warlord era (1912-27), the Great Leap Forward, the Cultural Revolution—repeatedly have prompted popular Western images of an ungovernable China in permanent chaos. But such images are soon stilled by a stable China in the throes of rapid development, as in the 1870s, the first decade of this century, the early 1930s, the 1950s, and the last decade. Each era of stability and growth has been heralded as the dawn of a "New China," which in turn evokes another set of popular images: an aroused dragon, the pragmatic and entrepreneurial Chinese, and the world belonging to China in the next century. At such moments, pundits sagely recall Napoleon's warning that an awakened China will shake the world. Yet, none of these promising beginnings has been sustained.

In the light of this history, a balanced and cautionary perspective is required that takes into account both continuities and discontinuities, the certainties and uncertainties, and the sources of optimism and caution about the Chinese future.

CONTINUITIES

The most important continuities arise from the cultural and historical legacies discussed above and the objective challenges of governing

China and pursuing a strategy of economic development congruent with the physical setting. With its huge population and size, China requires a political structure with six tiers: center, province, special district or metropolitan region, county, township, and village. And for some activities, three additional, intervening tiers exist. No country in the world has as many levels separating the top and bottom of the political pyramid. Designing the distribution of decision-making authority among these six levels—who is responsible for what—is one of the most challenging tasks of rule. Too much centralization prompts excessive bureaucracy and issuance of rules unsuited to diverse local conditions. Excessive decentralization risks fragmentation and a weak central government unable to perform its most basic responsibilities.

Further, the population must sustain itself on 60 percent of the cultivated acreage of the United States. That is, China must feed four times the population of the United States on much less agricultural land than the United States uses. Moreover, China is currently losing cultivated acreage through industrialization, urbanization, and desertification, and it cannot expand its cultivated acreage without massive capital investments in huge irrigation schemes. Chinese farmers currently till almost all the acreage that can be cultivated.

Chinese agriculture already is highly productive, when measured on a yield-per-hectare basis. Extensive use of irrigation, advanced seed strains, and chemical fertilizers make Chinese agriculture among the most productive in the world. Increases in per capita farm income therefore can only be secured by reducing the number of farmers and thereby increasing per capita productivity. To do this requires a massive shift from agricultural to non-agricultural employment. In the 1980s over one hundred million Chinese made this transition, and the number will climb in the 1990s.

DISCONTINUITIES

While China's huge population, inadequate amount of cultivated land, and geographic diversity establish enduring challenges of its governance, significant changes are occurring in these realms as well. In a very real sense, the 1980s and 1990s may be seen as the decades in which major, 3000-year-old, fundamental qualities of China changed. First, China's economy since time immemorial was based on agriculture. Peasants were largely self-sufficient. That is changing. Within a decade or two, less than half of the populace will be farmers, and most who till the soil will be bound into the market economy. Put another way, the majority of the population will live in urban areas and derive their income from industry, commerce, and services.

Second, urbanization and industrialization bring a more differentiated occupational structure and the growth of professions and professional associations.[1] Formal and informal communities of specialists, experts, and technicians both within and outside the Communist Party and government are influencing public policy. Many of the professions trace their origins to the 1920s and 1930s, if not before, and the ways they seek to influence the policy process grow out of the Chinese political culture and their particular pasts. While still operating in an authoritarian system and subject to political control, the professions show promise of achieving historically unprecedented political importance.

Third, throughout history, local and regional economies were largely self-sufficient.[2] China lacked a truly integrated, national economy. Transportation and communication facilities were weak. That too is changing. Television, telephones, airplanes, and unprecedented levels of population movement and migration are creating a level of national integration and interdependence unprecedented in Chinese history. To be sure, strong local, provincial, and regional barriers still exist. Ethnic, linguistic, and bureaucratic barriers separate one locality from another and give rise to various localist sentiments. And the nationalities that reside in China's border regions—Mongolians, Tibetans, Uygurs—are beginning to press for greater autonomy. But on balance, the Han people—some 90 percent of the populace—are being woven more tightly into a national economy and popular culture.

The fourth break with the past is China's integration into the world economy.[3] Over twenty percent of China's GNP now falls in the foreign trade sector. Fifteen years ago, the percentage was substantially less than ten percent. The rapid expansion of China's foreign trade is a major reason for China's growth in the 1980s and hence for its relatively smooth transition from a rural to an urban society.

Finally, the society and economy are placing unprecedented pressure on China's natural environment.[4] Air pollution, water pollution, contamination of soil through poor toxic waste management, deforestation, desertification, pollution of coastal waters, and acid rain are severe problems. To slow the rate of deterioration and to ensure adequate water supplies for industrial, urban, and agricultural use in China will require investments in the tens of billions of dollars. Given China's inevitable reliance on coal as its major fuel, to improve air quality will require billions of dollars of investment in use of clean coal technologies. And to reduce toxic emissions in a country where 80 percent of industrial waste and effluent discharge now goes untreated will necessitate yet additional tens of billions in investment. Never in its long history has China's ecology been under such intense pressure.

THE CERTAINTIES

Much about the Chinese future, as we note below, is uncertain. But some things are certain. Despite the vigorous—some would say draconian—family-planning program, China's population of 1.2 billion will continue to grow by 15-20 million people per year for the foreseeable future. Given the demographic realities and the yearnings of the populace for a higher standard of living, China's leaders must pursue a development strategy that yields high economic growth rates and employment opportunities for those exiting the rural sector. This imperative necessitates continuation of China's opening to the outside world—for technology, equipment, capital, and markets—and continuation of economic reform to increase efficiency and productivity. National, provincial, and local bureaucracies and leaders have acquired significant vested interests in the policies pursued during the past decade. Any effort to reverse those policies would encounter significant resistance and come at considerable cost.

There is another certainty: China will experience more social turmoil in the coming decade than it exhibited in the past fifteen years. Both the leaders of China and the leaders of Trilateral countries must not overreact and conclude that the social unrest is an indication of government failure. To the contrary, worker strikes, peasant riots, and student protests will signal that the government is less repressive, that government control of society has weakened, and that the state has reduced the range of social services it previously sought to provide: full urban employment, subsidized grain and cloth, subsidized housing, etc. Recent relaxation of controls over internal migration also means additional tens of millions of former rural residents will move to urban areas, living outside the previous control mechanisms. It stands to reason that China will not be exempt from the periodic social unrest that characterizes most developing countries. Protest and dissent should not be too swiftly placed in a Western context or likened to Western social movements.[5] When confronted with disorder, the challenge for both China's rulers and the outside world will be not to panic, not to conclude the regime's survival is at stake, but to place the unrest in its Chinese context and to respond accordingly. Thus, the Trilateral countries must not conclude that all protests indicate yearnings for democracy and the emergence of a civil society, while China's leaders should not judge that all dissidents wish to overthrow the regime. It is not certain however that either China's leaders or the Trilateral countries will exhibit this wisdom.

THE UNCERTAINTIES

While the turn to the outside and continued economic reform seem irreversible, much about the Chinese future is uncertain and problematic. Having overturned his previous succession arrangements centering on Hu Yaobang and Zhao Ziyang, Deng Xiaoping has sought in his last years to design an orderly succession centering on Party General Secretary and President of the PRC Jiang Zemin, supported by a collective leadership. But orderly successions have proven rare in communist systems and the Chinese past. Not until Deng has passed from the scene will it become clear who among the contenders has the requisites to be the preeminent leader of the country: ruthlessness, a lust for power, a vision relevant to the Chinese condition, and a network of personal ties that elicit support from the Party, army, and government both in Beijing and several key regions of the country. Indeed, not until Deng and the other remaining members of the Long March generation pass away will it become clear whether the institutions forged by the revolutionaries are sufficiently durable to survive them. Key to this will be the ability of the potential successors to contain the inevitable power struggles among them and to refrain from mobilizing supporters outside the Politburo and the apex of the system.

Fundamental institutional issues also await resolution. The appropriate distribution of authority between Beijing and the provinces is very much at issue, as is the relationship between the civilian and military sectors of the political system. The People's Liberation Army (PLA) is an instrument of the Party, not the government, and in reality reports directly to the Politburo.[6] Only at the apex of the political system do the civilian and military chains-of-command come together. There is no effective, in-depth civilian control of the military; the Ministry of National Defense is a paper organization. In the past decade, the PLA has converted many defense industries into producers of civilian goods, ranging from refrigerators to motor bikes. It has also entered world arms markets, with the incentive that it retains the foreign currency from these sales. The role of the PLA in the succession and its future relationship to the civilian sector are inescapable issues looming ahead.

The role of the Communist Party is also uncertain. Will it continue to justify its monopoly rule in accord with Marxist-Leninist theory as the vanguard of the proletarian revolution, a hollow claim in the light of the bankruptcy of Marxist-Leninist ideology and its own abandonment of class struggle? This claim is so hollow that it erodes the Party's legitimacy. But what other compelling theory can be propounded that justifies Party rule? What role can be carved out for it? Can it be transformed to represent the interests of the new elites—the urban middle class, professionals, entrepreneurs, and so on? That is, can it transform itself into a corporatist party, incorporating the natural elites of the various sectors of society and thereby playing an invaluable integrative role? Or, can it lumber along as an increasingly corrupt party machine dispensing jobs and patronage?

Another major institutional uncertainty is whether an effective central bank and an effective central revenue system can be created in China. No tasks are more immediately important in order to yield the central government effective instruments for guiding the economy through monetary and fiscal policies. For over a decade, however, China's central authorities have been attempting to create effective instruments of monetary and fiscal control, to no avail. Provincial authorities do not wish to surrender their ability to influence local banks to provide easy credit, and to retain an increasing percentage of government revenue.

Other unsettled questions concern the role of representative assemblies or parliaments (especially the National People's Congress) in the Chinese system and the issue of political participation. Can China's parliaments be enlivened and given meaningful policy-making powers? Would this make the government more responsible to popular will and help restore support for the regime? Could the bureaucracy be made accountable to the parliaments in order to control corruption and abuse of power?

Finally, what set of persuasive beliefs, if any, will the leaders propagate in order to unify and motivate the populace? Many thoughtful Chinese assert that the country now suffers from a spiritual vacuum brought on by the materialism of the Deng era. That is, Deng obtained popular support by pledging to raise the standard of living. He delivered on his promise. But many Chinese now want more. They wish their lives to have meaning. And in the absence of an official ideology, they are turning to religion: Christianity, Buddhism, Daoism, traditional folk religion.

Will Deng's successors attempt to fill the vacuum, as leaders in other countries, through the articulation of a nationalistic ideology, perhaps even deliberately drawing upon the Confucianist heritage? And would this ideology be a benign patriotism or an assertive nationalism?

We have identified a daunting list of institutional challenges that confront the regime: succession, central-provincial relations, civil-military relations, the role of the Communist Party, the banking and central revenue systems, the function of parliaments, and the ideology. Deng's failure vigorously to embark on political reforms is a major reason these uncertainties exist, and it is not clear when and how these complex problems will be addressed. But failure to address them guarantees that China at some point in the not-too-distant future will confront a political crisis.

CAUSES FOR OPTIMISM

Despite this political uncertainty, the economic prospects over the long run appear bright. The underlying factors for growth are in place: a high savings rate and hence a high rate of capital accumulation; an entrepreneurial populace whose talents have been unleashed; a basically sound natural resource endowment; the magnetic pull of the dynamic East Asian region; a favorable international environment; and the contributions of Taiwan, Hong Kong, and many ethnic Chinese in Southeast Asia, North America and Europe.

Indeed, the grounds for optimism should be placed in a broader historical perspective. Economic historians note that, despite the upheavals, the Chinese economy has demonstrated considerable vitality for over a century. Foreign aggression, civil war, and political blunders interfered with a robust growth trajectory. From this vantage point, China has returned to the path evident in the 1920s and 1930s, before the Japanese invasion and the turmoil of revolution interrupted the trend. Indeed, although starting from a low base, even with the Mao-inspired disruptions of the Great Leap Forward and Cultural Revolution, China's economic growth rate has averaged 7-8 percent not just for the last 15 years, but for the last 40 years. From this vantage point, Shanghai, Guangzhou, Tianjin, and Wuhan are reclaiming their leading positions among dynamic Asian cities that they lost during the Sino-Japanese War and the Communist revolution.

There is another reason for optimism. We have earlier noted that for over a century, China's political debates centered on what to borrow or reject from the West and what to preserve or discard from the Chinese past. These debates were often ideological, divisive, and debilitating. The issues at stake have by no means disappeared, but with the passing of the generation that came of age during China's May 4th movement of 1919—a movement that brought cultural and nationalistic issues to the fore and a generation that devoted their lives to warring over these issues—the agenda appears to have shifted somewhat.[7] An unprecedented pragmatism seems to characterize many in the next generation of leading intellectuals, who seem more interested in addressing the concrete issues of political and economic development.

THE COMPOSITE PICTURE

How, then, does one summarize the complex situation sketched in the previous pages? The answer requires a conceptual breakthrough. As already noted in our introductory chapter, China seems destined in the coming decade to combine qualities that traditionally have not co-existed in a rising power: territorially amorphous, politically messy, economically vibrant, socially unsettled, culturally proud, and internationally assertive. The challenge for the Trilateral countries is to cope with this kind of sprawling giant.

IV. Hong Kong, Taiwan, and "Greater China"

The division of China into three parts (Hong Kong, Taiwan and the PRC) greatly complicates attempts to integrate China into the international community, while providing further incentives for pursuing this integration. The past decade or so for the three parts of China has been a period of remarkable economic integration as well as economic dynamism. Economic integration has worked to the benefit of all three. Consider the following: In the 1980s, in any department store in the West, toys, dresses, men's wear and shoes all had labels stating "Made in Hong Kong" or "Made in Taiwan." In the 1990s these same labels all say "Made in China." A more accurate label would read: "Thought of in Taiwan, designed in Hong Kong, and constructed in China."

"GREATER CHINA"

The international community must be careful not to exaggerate or distort the political importance of this economic dynamism and integration. We turn later in this chapter to the complicated issues of Hong Kong and Taiwan. Here we turn to the notion of the emergence of a "Greater China."[1] To some, this phrase refers to all of mainland China, Taiwan, and Hong Kong. Other writers employ the term in a narrower sense to refer to Hong Kong, Taiwan, and the southeast mainland China coast from Guangdong and Fujian provinces to Shanghai. Yet other analysts use "Greater China" to encompass all ethnic Chinese, including in Southeast Asia and sometimes in North America and Europe.

Not a Useful Political or Cultural Concept

Let us quickly dismiss the more sensationalist portrayals of "Greater China" and then capture its more complex essence. "Greater China" most assuredly is not now and is not likely to become a single political entity.

Culturally too, the differences separating the many parts of "Greater China" are profound. Even the narrow definition embraces ethnic subgroups of Cantonese, Hokkienese, Taiwanese, Fukienese, Hakka, Shanghainese, and those from the Swatow region. All are Han Chinese, sharing a basically common written language and many common cultural attributes, but their spoken languages are quite distinctive, their identities are bound to their separate native places, and some vital aspects of their culture—such as cuisine, folk music, and marriage and burial customs—are different. On the mainland, significant cultural differences appear to be opening between those who remember the Mao era and those who matured in the Deng era. In recent decades, the non-mainland portions of "Greater China" have had much greater exposure to Western influence, and the ethnic Chinese of Southeast Asia and North America have begun the process of cultural assimilation. In some countries, such as Thailand, the Philippines, and the United States, second, third, and fourth generation Chinese have joined the national mainstreams, while in Indonesia or Malaysia assimilation has proceeded more slowly. To be sure, many ethnic Chinese outside of the mainland derive pride from the progress of the People's Republic, but this does not detract from their loyalty to their own country.

An effort is now underway among some leading intellectuals on the mainland, in Taiwan, in Hong Kong, and abroad to identify the core characteristics of Chinese civilization that bind all ethnic Chinese and to articulate a new ideology, rooted in Confucianism, that is germane to the modern world.[2] In light of the growing cultural diversity among ethnic Chinese, however, this effort seems doomed to futility unless it becomes an official orthodoxy backed by the power of the Chinese state. And such an effort would generate opposition as well as acceptance.

Convenient Shorthand for Four Developments

Thus "Greater China" is not a useful cultural or political concept. It is convenient shorthand for four interrelated economic and social developments.

It first of all refers to the increasingly intermeshed economies of Taiwan, Hong Kong, and mainland China, especially along the southeast coast. These three entities increasingly constitute a trans-state economic zone. Taiwan's and Hong Kong's economic successes drove China's growth, and now China's economic boom is an engine for growth in Hong Kong and Taiwan. Direct trade between the

People's Republic of China and the Republic of China (Taiwan) is illegal, but having Hong Kong play middleman has not hurt the Taiwanese-Beijing economic relationship: the total volume of their trade has jumped from $1.5 billion in 1987 to $14.3 billion in 1993. Over 5,000 Taiwanese enterprises have set up factories in the PRC. Some business firms in Taiwan are relocating entire factories to remote areas on the mainland to take advantage of cheap labor and more readily available natural resources.[3] More than 50 percent of the labor force of Hong Kong companies now works in mainland subsidiaries. Highways, ferries, hydrofoils and air routes link Hong Kong and the mainland coastal region. Hong Kong is China's top export market, primarily involved in generating re-exports. Hong Kong is also China's number one supplier, with 25.5 percent of total imports in 1992 (partly attributable to the increasing trade between China and Taiwan).[4] Table 3 in the next chapter indicates that almost 70 percent of foreign direct investment in China in 1992 came from Hong Kong, and almost 10 percent from Taiwan. (Japan, North America and Europe were well below Taiwan.) From an economic standpoint, China's three parts are growing ever closer together.

"Greater China" images are also aroused by the rise of multinational firms owned and managed by ethnic Chinese. Many of these firms are familial.[5] Some are based in Taiwan, others in Hong Kong, and yet others on the mainland or in Southeast Asia, but the property, factories, subsidiaries, and joint ventures of the typical firm are located throughout China and Southeast Asia. Many are conglomerates, but others concentrate on textiles, shipping, plastics, banking, or electronics. The largest of these firms are regularly on lists of the world's biggest corporations. Examples include the Evergreen Corporation and Taiwan Plastics in Taiwan, Hutcheson Corporation and Hopewell Corporation in Hong Kong, China International Trust and Investment Corporation (CITIC) based on the mainland, and C & P of Thailand. Each of these firms has been developed by a particular extraordinary Chinese entrepreneur. Despite their size and listing on the Taipei, Hong Kong, and/or Bangkok stock markets, most of these firms remain rather opaque, their financing and management practices not well understood. Chinese business networks are being grafted onto American corporate networks, the Japanese *keiretsu*, and the Korean *chaebols*. Through joint ventures, and hiring of ethnic Chinese by foreign corporations, foreign corporations are being incorporated into the Chinese environment, rather than being kept apart from it. In this regard, China has opened itself to foreign direct investment to a greater extent than many other Asian economies.

"Greater China" also involves the formation of formal and informal networks among ethnic Chinese professionals ranging from architects to environmentalists, historians, philosophers, and zoologists. Drawn together by shared intellectual interests, these professionals transcend their political differences and seek to advance their fields of specialization, especially on the mainland. These associations are apolitical, but in many respects their formation challenges the existing political order. They seek a degree of autonomy and an opportunity for interaction that the governments in Taipei and Beijing are not yet eager to accept. In this sense, their rise promotes political liberalization. These professions, of course, are integrated into their worldwide professional networks as well: doctors, lawyers, physicists, and so on. Thus, we are seeing the emergence of ethnic Chinese professional networks and the incorporation of these associations into global professional groupings. And their international standards are becoming the standards of the profession in mainland China, Taiwan, and Hong Kong.

Finally, "Greater China" images are aroused by the resurgence of an international nether world of secret societies, gangs, and traffickers of drugs, weapons, prostitutes, illegal migrants, and stolen merchandise. They bribe and have connections with local officials, especially the police, military, and customs service. Their reappearance along the China coast echoes earlier periods in Chinese history, and their origins and methods of operation can be traced to the pre-Communist era.

A careful examination of "Greater China" suggests the Trilateral countries do not confront the rise of a cohesive, coordinated, and slightly conspiratorial entity. Rather, the economic dynamism means that many Chinese bureaucracies, corporations, and individuals are acquiring considerable amounts of capital. Quite naturally, they are investing a significant portion of their capital in locales where the rates of return promise to be high, they feel comfortable, and they know how to operate. Substantially smaller sums are invested for sentimental and patriotic reasons and to bring honor to ancestors. Personal relationships (or *quanxi*) are important in facilitating business transactions in this Chinese world, but this is a natural reaction to the absence of an effective legal system to enforce contracts. In such a vacuum, trust, friendship, and a sense of mutual obligations are the necessary ingredients to make promises credible and business transactions viable.

Growth of Regionalism

A trans-state economic zone exists in south China, with the Hong Kong dollar circulating in Guangdong and the Taiwan dollar in Fujian province. Similarly, Yunnan and Guizhou provinces in the southwest are forming links with Burma, Thailand, and Laos. Korean trade and investments are expanding in Shandong. A trans-state economic zone is arising in the northeast, linking Manchuria with the Russian Far East, Japan, Mongolia and the two Koreas. And in China's far northwest, Xinjiang is forging extensive commercial ties with Kazakhstan and the other Central Asian Republics. In short, different border regions are developing distinctive sets of trading relations with the many countries on the Chinese periphery.

Meanwhile, within the country, the various macro-regions are pursuing somewhat different development strategies. Four of these regions, which are defined by China's river and railroad systems, are along the coast: (1) the Pearl River delta, embracing Guangzhou and Hong Kong; (2) the lower Yangtze basin, centering on Nanjing and Shanghai; (3) the North China plain, traversed by the Yellow River and focused on Beijing and Tianjin; and (4) the Manchurian corridor from Harbin to Dalian. These regions—especially the Pearl River delta and the lower Yangtze—have export-led growth strategies. But the North China and Manchurian regions, with substantial, pre-existing industrial bases, are somewhat more desirous to protect their state-owned industries and hence are attracted to import-substitution growth strategies. Meanwhile the macro-regions of the interior—the middle Yangtze and its urban center of Wuhan, the Sichuan basin of the upper Yangtze and its urban centers of Chengdu and Chongqing, and the northwest involving Xian and Lanzhou—face severe transportation constraints that limit their access to foreign markets. Their available strategies, which inescapably lead to lower growth rates than the coast, entail a greater focus on rural and consumer-led growth, attracting capital from the coast, reliance on central government subsidies, encouraging their populace to seek employment in more prosperous regions and remit funds home, and even investing some of their own funds in China's high-growth regions.

In sum, a many-dimensional "Greater China" is rising that embraces both the mainland and Chinese worlds outside the mainland. At the same time, the political center on the mainland is experiencing an erosion and fragmentation of its authority. The Trilateral countries—to return to a constant theme in this report—face the conceptual challenge of understanding and coping with this complexity.

HONG KONG AND TAIWAN

While relations among the mainland, Taiwan and Hong Kong ultimately will be settled by the three governments and their peoples, the Trilateral countries will influence the situation and affect the course of events.

Hong Kong

For the Chinese, Hong Kong is a painful reminder of their humiliations at the hands of the West. The Communist rulers allowed its continued separate existence after 1949 because it afforded China access to the outside world during a period of enforced isolation. As China opened its doors in the Deng era, Hong Kong played an important role in China's development, particularly that of its southern coastal regions. Hong Kong, therefore, conjures up in microcosm the contradictory images many Chinese have of Western Europe, North America and Japan as sources of cultural pollution and exploitation and as forces for economic change and access to superior technology.

These contradictory images have not helped in China's protracted negotiations over Hong Kong's political development, which have been rocky at best. The People's Republic wants to establish its supremacy in the economic and political life of Hong Kong while not destroying Hong Kong's value as an economic dynamo. A series of arrangements have been established to provide for a special administrative region for 50 years following Hong Kong's return to China in 1997. These include the Joint Declaration, the 1984 Sino-British agreement on Hong Kong's future, and the Basic Law (the post-1997 constitution drawn up by Beijing in 1990) setting election modalities for the head of the Special Administrative Region and the Legislative Chamber (Legco). But there are different interpretations of the letter and spirit of these arrangements by China, the United Kingdom, and various groups in Hong Kong.

Beijing's disenchantment with British Governor Chris Patten, who has sought to expand the electorate and reinforce the rule of law prior to reversion, has led to a marked deterioration in Sino-British relations. Patten has described his policies to the House of Commons Foreign Affairs Committee (in January 1994) as "not about an eleventh-hour acceleration of democracy. If, against Chinese demands, we were to be doing that, for example increasing the number of directly elected seats (in the Legco), you could charge the government with seeking to accelerate democracy. As it happens we have decided to accept the pace of democratization proposed by China and set out in the Basic Law and what we are attempting to do is ensure that the process is credible. That is a different enterprise, perhaps a less heroic enterprise, but an important one nonetheless...." The authorities in Beijing, however, see Patten's innovations and the way they were proposed as a violation of the spirit of the agreements and China's prerogatives. The ensuing dispute has left many Hong Kongers and foreigners concerned about the future of the territory following 1997.

One reason for optimism about Hong Kong's future is that mainland government agencies and corporations have invested so much in the territory and reaped so much profit in return that the central government has great incentive to maintain Hong Kong's economy and society, particularly once reversion has occurred. Hong Kong in effect has extended its economic system into southern China, moving outward and fuzzing the "boundary" between Hong Kong and the rest of China. A good example of this interdependence is in the monetary area. The Hong Kong and Shanghai Bank estimates that $2 billion in Hong Kong banknotes, about 30 per cent of the total, circulate on the mainland (principally Guangdong), up from 24 per cent of the total in 1989. This growing interdependence of Guangdong and Hong Kong constrains the distant authorities in Beijing and London in guiding the destiny of this trans-state economic region. The centrality of Hong Kong to economic growth in southern China and of southern China in Chinese national economic development also gives Hong Kong bargaining leverage with Beijing.

Will the Chinese strictly adhere to the basic agreement for 50 years after 1997? Although there are reasons for some optimism, the political context will change significantly in the coming years. Despite its special status, Hong Kong will be one of several areas competing for influence within a broader Chinese framework. Its economic role as a center for finance and other services will also face stiffer competition from Shanghai and possibly other Chinese centers, which might try to use their political influence in Beijing to improve their relative economic positions vis-à-vis Hong Kong. It would be in China's interest to have multiple competing centers of economic dynamism. It is not in its interest, however, that the rise of other economic centers come at the expense of Hong Kong.

Because of Hong Kong's status as a colony before 1997, the Trilateral countries have a multitude of special arrangements and obligations to Hong Kong, such as separate textile quota arrangements. Such obligations could not be transferred to other parts of China should the special administrative arrangements for Hong Kong not be honored or if Beijing sought such transfer. Instead, they would be lost. On this and other matters, given the long association of Hong Kong with the West, China's treatment of Hong Kong will have an important bearing on China's relations with the Trilateral countries.

Taiwan

Beyond the Hong Kong issue, Sino-Taiwanese relations present even greater challenges, both for China and for the international community. Despite increasing economic integration with the mainland, the government in Taipei is reluctant to engage in direct, official political contacts with the leaders in Beijing, and is increasingly dissatisfied with its ambiguous international status. This dissatisfaction puts the international community in something of a bind, recognizing on the one hand that the Taiwan issue is best left to the officials and people in Taiwan and the mainland to resolve, but on the other hand having a vested interest in a peaceful resolution of the issue. Even further, Trilateral countries have important obligations concerning Taiwan.

The sparring in Taiwan/China relations was clearly visible in the conflicting remarks made by the leaders of the PRC and the Kuomintang at the APEC meeting in Seattle in November 1993. Taiwan's Minister of Economic Affairs, P.K. Chiang, caused quite a stir with his references to "...two sovereign nations across the Taiwan Strait," and by mentioning that Taiwan is now pursuing a "...transitional two-Chinas policy." Meanwhile, Chinese President Jiang Zemin consistently referred to Taiwan as a "province" of China.

It is ironic that these conflicting comments were made at the Asia Pacific Economic Cooperation meeting, to which both China and Taiwan belong, and which has been hailed as one of the few multilateral organizations that has managed to successfully circumvent this intractable problem. It is also noteworthy that it is on the basis of economic cooperation that China and Taiwan are able to meet and work together, even if not in perfect harmony. Already, economic considerations seem to have tempered some of the rhetoric emanating from Beijing on the Taiwan issue. Shang Mingqing, a senior official at the Office of Taiwan Affairs in the State Council, recently said: "I should not say we have acquiesced in slowing down the talks (about reunification), but there is nothing we can do. It largely depends on them (the Taiwanese government) whether they want to sit and talk."[6] This is a far cry from previous Chinese statements about reunification. In the past, China promised direct military action if Taiwan even thought about "independence." Beijing officials now admit that Taiwan is in a position to dictate the pace of integration and eventual reunification.[7]

The fluid political situation in Taiwan makes it unclear how Taiwan will actually play these cards. In the recent past, the Kuomintang (KMT) has advocated "one country with two political entities." However, the gradual accession to power of indigenous Taiwanese, the "Taiwanization" of the mainland element that fled to Taiwan in 1949, and the gradual process of democratization have given powerful political expression to the call to abandon the claim to be the "lawful government of China" and seek international recognition as an autonomous government.

This political shift was reflected in the recent elections, when the KMT adopted some of the independence-minded Democratic Progress Party's (DPP) platform, in order to sustain its slim majority—47 percent to the DPP's 41 percent. The rise of the DPP could put the Trilateral countries in a particularly awkward position, as one of the main tenets of its platform is Taiwanese reentry into the United Nations. (The UN is quite aware that this is not even a possibility, and the General Assembly has refused to consider Taiwan's bid for membership.)

Yet, should there be a DPP victory, it is unlikely that Taiwan will declare independence. Economic integration has affected the DPP's political orientation as well. The strong backers of the DPP work in small and medium-sized businesses, which have been the biggest investors in the mainland. Despite official party rhetoric, they are now cautious about outright independence. They have no desire to jeopardize their already profitable investments. A Taiwanese bid for independence under present circumstances would be in no one's interest, and would jeopardize all the economic and political gains that have been won.

POLICY IMPLICATIONS FOR TRILATERAL COUNTRIES

Clearly, the division of China presents one of the most vexing set of challenges for outside countries in their relations with China. While the future of relations between Taiwan and the mainland is ultimately a matter for the two sides to decide, outsiders do have legitimate interests in maintaining an economically stable and peaceful Taiwan. The Trilateral nations should not challenge the "one China" claim; but neither should they lead Beijing to believe it could successfully apply pressure on Taiwan on issues that would risk Taiwan's stability and prosperity. In the final analysis, the Trilateral nations should coordinate policy to sustain the delicate status quo in the region, and to make it as easy as possible for the PRC and Taiwan to sustain their implicit "strategy of procrastination."

However, within this framework, the Trilateral nations can take several steps that may help maintain the regional equilibrium. Taiwan's 21 million people and their $210 billion GNP cannot be ignored or simply forgotten. There should be acknowledgement of Taiwan's accomplishments, both because of its dynamic economic growth and because of its concerted efforts at democratization. The Trilateral countries have a vested interest in an ongoing healthy economic relationship between China and Taiwan. Many of Taiwan's firms—with over $10 billion invested in the mainland—are exporting to North America, Europe and Japan. Therefore the Trilateral nations must be sure to remain engaged economically and politically with both Taiwan and the mainland. There should be a particular effort to strengthen U.S.-PRC ties. A strong United States presence will facilitate stable relations between the PRC and Taiwan. Conversely, tensions in the U.S.-PRC relationship will surely adversely affect relations between the PRC and Taiwan, as well as relations between the mainland and other Trilateral countries.[8]

The Trilateral countries can also satisfy Taiwan's desire for greater recognition through Taiwan's already successful membership in the APEC group. This could be a particularly appealing route, now that APEC is acknowledged as a legitimate political entity in the region. President Li Teng-hui's recent meetings with both President Suharto of Indonesia and President Ramos of the Phillipines reflect the new recognition and respect that Taiwan has gained from neighboring countries. Through APEC, Taiwan can increase her ties with all its members, and perhaps even find some new ground with the PRC. Some have commented on the utility of APEC as a neutral forum in which the three parts of China can gather to discuss their problems. Encouraging further engagement in APEC will allow the three to underline and recognize the importance of working out their differences in the name of continuing economic prosperity and peace.

The successful compromise worked out for the three ethnic

Chinese entities to enjoy membership in APEC should be drawn on when incorporating the Chinese Economic Area (CEA) into other regional and international organizations. The next goal should be the World Trade Organization (WTO). Integrating the CEA into the WTO is a top Trilateral priority in general, and it could be particularly effective in encouraging peaceful and productive relations between the three entities.

On the negative side of the equation, Trilateral countries should take great care to avoid policies that might tip the political balance among the three. Among the chief concerns are Trilateral exports of clearly offensive weapons to Taiwan. Many Trilateral countries may be tempted by Taiwan's booming arms market, and the United States has legislation mandating such exports. The full consequences of such sales must be carefully considered. They may provoke destabilizing exports from China to other regional trouble spots. They may disturb the balance of power in the Taiwan Strait and encourage the PRC to redress the balance through arms purchases of its own. Or, in contrast, they may help maintain the military balance and sustain Taiwan's self-confidence so that it will continue to broaden its contacts with the mainland. Clearly, this is a sufficiently subtle matter that sales must be carefully calibrated and not made for domestic economic or political purposes.

The Trilateral countries should also be aware of the effect of their relations with China on Beijing's relations with Hong Kong and Taiwan. If Trilateral countries adopt policies which reduce trade with China, either intentionally or through a deterioration in relations with Beijing, Beijing might feel freer to force a solution on Taiwan and Hong Kong.[9] Trilateral policy should be to help prevent such crises from ever occurring. Cooperation among the Trilateral nations is important for this, along with a corresponding recognition of the limited effect of any of our actions on events in the CEA.

V. THE CHINESE ECONOMY: GLOBAL AND REGIONAL DIMENSIONS

The development of a vigorous market economy in China, a country of 1.2 billion people, is surely one of the most significant events in recent history. Whether measured using current exchange rates or on a purchasing-power-parity basis, China's GNP is rising at an unprecedented pace, outstripping even the miraculous growth of the "East Asia Tigers" and reaching annual growth figures of 12 and 13 percent.[1]

Much of this economic dynamism is the result of China's participation in the international economy. China's position as the world's tenth largest exporter in 1992 put it just behind the core industrialized nations. (For comparison, Japan was the world's ninth largest exporter when it became a GATT member in 1955). Much of China's trading success is due to a pragmatic, outward-oriented strategy focused on increasing exports and attracting foreign investments. China has been building economic ties with nations that promise to be the best partners. It has also sought to diversify sources of investment capital, science, and technology so as not to be overly dependent on any single source of outside supply. This has meant greatly expanded ties with the dynamic Asia-Pacific region, but Europe and North America have also been beneficiaries of China's economic development. For example, in November while Boeing workers in Seattle were displaying their factory to President Jiang Zemin, a representative of one of Boeing's best customers, German Chancellor Helmut Kohl was in China blessing several billion dollars worth of contracts and letters of intent from his Chinese hosts.

CHINA'S ECONOMIC STRATEGIES

Unlike the rise of other East Asian developing countries, such as Japan and South Korea, China's development in the earlier stages was not based on an export-led growth strategy. The outward-looking development strategy is the most recent of three different economic development and national security strategies that Chinese leaders have pursued since the establishment of the People's Republic in 1949.2 In the 1950s Mao Zedong and his lieutenants in large measure emulated the Stalinist model of economic development and sought security through alliance with the Soviet Union. Thus Mao nationalized industry, collectivized agriculture, sought Soviet aid, mobilized high rates of savings, concentrated investments in heavy industry, neglected the service sector, and embarked on five-year plans.

In the 1960s and early 1970s, largely due to the Sino-Soviet dispute and continued Sino-American animosity, Mao sought a distinctive path to a socialist modernity, championing both national and local self-reliance, continued high rates of capital accumulation, and mobilization of the populace through ideological appeals. Defiance of both the United States and the U.S.S.R. necessitated increases in defense expenditures. Fearing war, Mao directed investments toward the southwest and the interior, leaving a legacy of large, isolated, and inefficient state enterprises.

Each of these strategies was abandoned due to glaring deficiencies. The Stalinist model was unsuited to the Chinese condition, particularly because of its neglect of agriculture. Nor did the Soviet Union provide the level of economic and security assistance that the Chinese had hoped for. The 1960s model of self-reliance exhausted the energies of the populace without providing sufficient reward, and the simultaneous opposition to Moscow and Washington left China weak, isolated, and endangered. Further, massive policy errors during the Great Leap Forward, with resulting widespread famine and death, and the chaos and violence of the Cultural Revolution and its aftermath disillusioned and alienated substantial portions of the population.

Except for the worst years of Maoist economic mismanagement, the economy continued to grow, albeit in a distorted manner. High capital accumulation was the main reason for growth, but toward the end of the Maoist period, the rate of return on investment was diminishing rapidly. Maintaining a high savings rate would no longer sustain rapid growth. Moreover, during the 1960s and 1970s, the outward-directed economies of Japan, South Korea, and Taiwan soared. Instead of being at the forefront, China lagged behind the other East Asian economies.

As he ascended to power in 1977-79, Deng Xiaoping enunciated three overarching and somewhat contradictory themes to remedy the situation. These have remained the hallmarks of his rule: open

China's doors to the outside world, reform the economy, and preserve Communist political power.[3] More gradually, Deng and his associates, always confronting an array of skeptics and opponents, developed a strategy of reform. The basic elements were to give primacy to economic over political reform, secure popular support through improvement in standards of living, move from rural reform to urban reform, move from the easy to the more difficult reforms, build constituencies in favor of reform (especially cultivating support among provincial officials), use foreign support and external agreements as levers to support the reform program, give bureaucratic opponents a stake in the reform process, and—except for a period of indecisiveness in the spring of 1989 prior to June 4—crack down harshly and swiftly on dissidents.

Beyond the general direction and broad strategy, the reform process has been experimental, somewhat ad hoc, and incremental. The reforms have unfolded in phases. In the late 1970s and early 1980s, they focused on rural reform and on the initial opening to the outside world, through entrance into the World Bank and the IMF, creation of the special economic zones (SEZs), and invitations to foreign corporations to establish joint ventures.

By making the decollectivization of agriculture his first step, Deng immediately enlivened a sector of the economy that employed 80 percent of China's workforce, doubling farmers' incomes and paving the way for rapid agricultural growth. This in turn spurred the development of light industry. During this period, the government was able to keep inflation sufficiently low, making China attractive for foreign investors.

By 1984-85, the focal point had moved to the urban sector, where the major obstacles to growth and market reform were the inefficient state-owned enterprises. In the initial stage, the huge, state-owned enterprises continued to be subsidized as inefficient units of production. Management reforms and technological innovations were undertaken to improve their productivity, and some price reforms in the state-dominated sectors were implemented. But the leaders also allowed the urban private sector to grow rapidly, and the state-owned firms began to produce goods outside the plan for sale on the market. Thus, while the absolute size of the state and planned sector remained roughly the same, its relative importance diminished. By 1988-89, the stage was set for a more direct reform of state enterprises, necessitating privatization and allowing inefficient ones to go bankrupt. However, inflation resulting from an overheated economy and price reform, the demonstrations of spring 1989, and the ensuing brutal crackdown altered the political balance of forces and postponed further reforms.

After stalling in 1989-92, the pace of reform again quickened following Deng Xiaoping's call for more rapid growth, greater openness, and stepped-up reform during his tour of southern China in 1992. The aging leader then received much needed political support when the fourteenth Congress of the Chinese Communist Party (CCP), the Eighth National People's Congress in March 1993, and the Third Plenum of the CCP's Fourteenth Central Committee in November 1993 all endorsed his policies. The Third Plenum in particular may be seen as decisive; it endorsed major reforms of the banking and financial systems, privatization of state-owned firms, and introduction of capital and securities markets. All these measures accelerated movement toward a genuine market economy.

CHINA'S TRADE AND INVESTMENT SUCCESSES

The policies of the Deng era have already made China more economically interdependent with the world than is usually imagined. Export volumes grew at an average annual rate of over 10 percent between 1980 and 1991. Exports now account for more than 20 percent of China's GNP (based on current exchange rate calculations), a significantly higher percentage than for either the United States or Japan and comparable to levels for the major economies of Western Europe. Forty percent of these exports come from enterprises established through foreign investment. As imports have also boomed, total trade in 1992 amounted to $165 billion (2.2 percent of world trade), and the figure rose dramatically to $195 billion in 1993.

China's exports have burgeoned in such labor-intensive products as clothing, shoes and toys. More recently, it has begun to export such products as personal computers and other electronic goods. China's imports offer an opportunity for industries in the Trilateral countries. The composition of imports has changed as China has developed. In the early 1980s, the Chinese sought large turn-key plants, and then equipment for renovation of existing plants. As disposable incomes rose late in the decade so too did the importation of consumer goods. China now is or soon will become one of the world's leading markets for high-tech goods, transportation and telecommunications equipment, power plants, pollution abatement equipment, and services.

China will also become a significant oil importer. Currently the fifth largest producer in the world, surging growth has increased the demand above China's domestic supply, making it a net petroleum importer in 1994 for the first time. This has both economic and strategic dimensions, as noted in the next chapter.

China's global impact is also being felt in world capital markets. The desire to participate in China's dynamic internal market, the establishment of manufacturing facilities to use China's plentiful labor, the first steps to make its currency convertible, and attractive bond offers on international credit markets, are all making China a magnet for foreign capital. In particular, over the past two years, foreign investment into China has boomed. The numbers are presented in Table 1 and examined in more detail in Tables 2 and 3. Contracted foreign investment for 1992 equalled the accumulated totals of the previous 13 years, and another huge increase was registered in 1993. China has become the world's largest beneficiary of direct foreign investment.

TABLE 1
Inflow of Foreign Investment to China, 1979-93
(billions of US$)

	Contracted	Implemented
1979-82	7.0	1.8
1983	1.9	0.9
1984	2.9	1.4
1985	6.3	2.0
1986	3.3	2.2
1987	4.3	2.6
1988	6.2	3.7
1989	6.3	3.8
1990	7.0	3.8
1991	12.4	4.7
1992	58.7	11.3
1993	100.0	20.0

Source: See N.T. Wang, "The Role of Foreign Direct Investment in Reform and Development in China," Institute Reports, East Asian Institute, Columbia University (New York: December 1993), p. 10. Calculated from *Zhongguo Tongji Zhaiyao* (Statistical Abstract of China) *1993* (Beijing: Statistical Publishing Association of China, 1993), p. 106.

Note: The figures include foreign direct investment and other foreign investment as defined in Table 2. In 1992, foreign direct investment accounted for 97.5% of the total. Preliminary estimates for 1993 are based on news releases for the first half or first eight months of the year by the Ministry of Foreign Trade and Economic Cooperation.

TABLE 2
Inflow of Foreign Investment to China, by Form, 1992
(percent of total implemented inflows)

Foreign Direct Investment	97.5
Joint Venture	*54.2*
Contractual Joint Venture	*18.8*
Wholly Foreign-Owned Enterprises	*6.4*
Joint Development Projects	*1.8*
Other Foreign Investment	2.5
Leasing	*0.4*
Compensation Trade	*1.5*
Assembly	*0.6*
Total	**100.0**

Source: Same as Table 1. Wang took the table from the same underlying source (p. 107) as cited in Table 1.

TABLE 3
Inflow of Foreign Direct Investment to China, by Source, 1992
(percent of total)

	Contracted	Implemented
Hong Kong*	69.0	68.2
Taiwan	9.5	9.5
Macau	2.6	1.8
Japan	3.7	6.4
United States	5.4	4.6
Canada		0.5
Germany, France, UK, Italy		1.7
Singapore	1.7	1.1
South Korea		1.1
Thailand	1.2	0.8
Total	**100.0**	**100.0**

Sources: Same as Table 1. Wang calculated the table from *Guoji Shangbao* (International Commerce), no. 4, 1993, cited in *China Newsletter*, no. 105 (July-August 1993), pp. 19-21. The "implemented" shares for Canada, the four largest EU countries, and South Korea are from a matching table in Kiichiro Fukasaku and Mingyuan Wu, "China as a Leading Pacific Economy," Technical Papers No. 89, OECD Development Centre (Paris: OECD, November 1993), p. 43.

*A portion of the Hong Kong share represents "round tripping": some domestic Chinese investors channel their investments through foreign intermediaries (usually located in Hong Kong) in order to qualify for the treatment accorded to foreign investment. See Nicholas Lardy, *China in the World Economy* (Washington, DC: Institute for International Economics, 1994).

This rapid inflow has been accompanied by substantial loans from the World Bank (including from IDA, its soft-loan window), making China the largest World Bank borrower in 1992 and 1993. It is likely to remain so for several more years, and is an extensive borrower from the Asian Development Bank as well. The inflow of capital from these institutions, as well as bilateral yen loans from Japan, help fund the infrastructural projects that China's development requires.

THE CHALLENGES OF CHINA'S ECONOMIC MIRACLE

China's economic achievements present new opportunities and challenges for China and for the Trilateral countries. The development of economic institutions in China has not kept pace with her rapid growth, leaving her economic development and trade insufficiently regulated. Political difficulties, including the weakening of central direction and political factionalism, have exacerbated problems of control. This poses serious dangers for China's domestic economy and for its principal trade and investment partners. Four areas of greatest concern stand out: its overheated economy, the growing disparities in development between coastal and interior regions, the inhospitality of its domestic market for foreign trade and investment, and surging and potentially disruptive exports. We examine each of these in turn.

The Overheated Economy

Inflation is a major threat to China's economic expansion (along with unemployment and an inadequate central government revenue base). With only fledgling financial and monetary institutions, China has had great difficulty in regulating its growth cycle. The result has been constant "zig-zags" since the Deng reforms began. Currently China is in one of its most potent booms. Yet there is great danger of excessive inflation that could hurt the additional market reforms planned for the future, including the reorganization and strengthening of the banking, tax and currency-exchange systems. This could jeopardize China's early entry into the GATT.

Inflation also poses serious challenges to social stability. Indeed, the economic backdrop to Tiananmen Square was an inflationary trend that caused students and workers to protest. Zhu Rongji, senior vice premier in charge of the economy, recognized these dangers last year and implemented a 16-point austerity program designed to cool the economy. However, these measures caused such a backlash in both Beijing and the rich coastal Special Economic Zones that China's leaders decided to de-emphasize the program, despite the dangers of excessive growth. The consequences may be further aggravation of inflationary pressures and over-expansion in specific economic sectors. The cost of living in 1993 rose 14.5 percent for the nation as a whole, according to the official statistics, and nearly 20 percent for medium-sized and large cities.

The diversity of the country and the differential effects of growth in urban and rural areas greatly complicate the task of controlling inflationary pressures. Although inflation is higher in the cities, unemployment is also high, making a quick solution to these problems politically infeasible. Likewise, state industries, which still represent more than half of industrial production, are heavily dependent on an easy supply of government credit. Yet the needed streamlining of bloated state enterprises is likely to increase unemployment and strain social stability, and it was these enterprises that were most vociferous in attacking the 1993 austerity program. Zhu recently commented: "What we want is a soft landing while the growth rate is gradually lowered. If we drastically reduced the growth rate, we would have to pay the cost of social stability."[4]

At the same time, rural areas are suffering both from the rising cost of living and insufficient government revenues, forcing cuts in rural subsidies. Last year when the government distributed IOUs (promises of later payment) instead of money in return for grain, it touched off a rash of peasant protests. Many peasants withheld grain they were obligated to sell to the government, setting off a consumer hoarding binge and forcing the government to take special measures to avert food shortages.

The control of growth and inflation is a delicate but necessary task. China is at a critical point. This year the government renewed its efforts to control monetary growth and scale back last year's 12.8 percent GNP growth to a more manageable 9 percent. Banking, trade, and foreign exchange reforms are being planned. But it is not at all clear what a longer-term sustainable growth rate might be.

Coastal-Interior Disparities

Deng's economic reforms have focused on the coastal regions, where lower taxes, infrastructural development, and other favorable elements entice investors. In theory, the wealth from the coast will trickle inland. This, in fact, is happening from such areas as Guangdong and Fujian, where newly rich coastal entrepreneurs are beginning to invest inland. In part encouraged by government exhortation but also responding to economic incentives, these entrepreneurs are aware that the coastal areas can benefit from interior markets and are dependent upon the interior for many raw materials.

The more general trend, however, is a growing economic disparity between the coast and the interior. On the average, people in the interior have only a fraction of the annual income of their counterparts in the SEZs. At least 90 million peasants in the interior live at subsistence levels. Not surprisingly, this has generated both resentment toward the richer coastal areas and massive internal migration, introducing a wide range of social problems. In the coastal cities, native inhabitants resent the newly arrived immigrants who are often unemployed, appear to depress wages, and place enormous new burdens on the existing urban infrastructure.

For all the economic benefits associated with the SEZs, the tax system built around them has added to these problems. The coastal areas have negotiated a political compromise that allows them to retain their profits. This reduces the central revenue base. At the same time, the poorer, weaker inland areas remain largely dependent on central government largesse. Thus, as stated earlier, tax reforms to redistribute the country's new wealth more equitably remain an imperative.

Protected Domestic Markets

While China has made remarkable progress in economic liberalization, foreigners still confront multiple market access barriers, especially in the service sector. Numerous regulations and practices are designed to protect inefficient state enterprises and exploit foreign capital, or have those effects. Export requirements are frequently imposed and "price-gouging" is common.

It was expected that China's moves toward a convertible currency would relieve the price-gouging problem. However, the impact of devaluation and the phasing out of exorbitantly priced foreign exchange certificates in 1993-94 was counterbalanced by illicit price hikes of 50 percent or more for foreigners.[5] A variety of other problems have also encouraged foreign investors to begin to organize to register their grievances in a more systematic manner with the authorities. But they are fighting an uphill battle, for until China begins serious privatization of the state enterprises, there will continue to be strong political pressures to contain competition. Effective laws to govern foreign investment and business activities are needed to deal with illicit price-gouging and similar activities.

Disruptive Exports

Deng's reform policies recognized the potential of the Chinese economy to produce and export competitive products, thus following a familiar export-oriented East Asian growth strategy. In particular, his trade policy was based on producing low-cost, labor-intensive goods, such as textiles, toys, and shoes, and in more recent times more technologically sophisticated products such as electronic goods. As a result, China's exports increased at twice the rate of world trade growth in the 1980s and early 1990s. The pace and magnitude of China's export successes in themselves create social adjustment problems for trading partners, but what makes them especially controversial is that they have often been accompanied by unscrupulous practices that have violated established international trade law and practice. These include subsidies, unrealistic pricing, falsification of documents, copyright and trademark violations, and the use of prison labor. The lack of an established legal system based on transparency and objective enforcement compound these problems.

The result has been innumerable trade disputes that have sometimes led to formal measures to restrict imports from China. The European Commission is taking anti-dumping actions against Chinese steel and chemical products. In January 1994, the United States threatened a major tariff increase on Chinese textiles in response to convincing evidence of illicit Chinese transshipments, overshipments, and false labeling. The U.S. Trade Representative has placed China on the "Priority Watch" list for its inadequate enforcement of intellectual property protection. Even Japan felt compelled to impose anti-dumping penalties on some Chinese steel production, its first ever resort to such penalties.

Trade surpluses are not the primary problem. Since the economic reforms began, China has more often sustained global trade deficits than had surpluses, although in recent years it has built an enormous bilateral surplus with the United States and some European countries. The major concern should center on China's commitment to adhere to internationally accepted trade rules and practices and, even when committed, its ability to enforce appropriate standards. China currently lacks the machinery to contain disruptive export surges that may threaten its economic partners. These issues have important implications for China's prospective membership in the GATT.

POLICY IMPLICATIONS

At the present time, there is a "get rich quick" mentality among many Chinese and foreigners doing business with China. This mentality emphasizes short-term profits and "exploitation" in the worst sense of the term, rather than responsible and sustainable development. The Trilateral governments have also been affected by this approach; the visits of political leaders usually focus on stimulating economic interaction without sufficient regard to the longer-term implications. Foreign businesses and the governmental leaders who support them are agents of change, but they need to be sensitive to the impact of their activity on China's long-term stability and development. If foreigners are later blamed for massive environmental and social problems associated with irresponsible development, this would not only be a tragedy for China's people and their environment, but would also be very damaging to the longer-term relationship of China with the Trilateral countries.

As stated at the outset of this report, we regard China's economic development as an enormous opportunity for mankind to lift a large share of the world's population from conditions of poverty to economic well-being. But this opportunity imposes heavy responsibilities on both China and its economic partners to ensure that this be done in a responsible and sustainable manner and in conformity with the internationally agreed-upon rules for international economic interaction. For this reason, it is a high priority to involve China in an active way in the major global and regional institutions where issues of trade, economic and social development, and the environment are being examined. For example, membership in the World Bank and the IMF has led the Chinese government to refine and release economic data long classified as state secrets, helping economic transparency.

Membership in GATT/WTO

China has joined most major international and regional organizations except for the GATT, to which it is seeking entry. The Trilateral countries have an important stake in assuring the commitment of China and Taiwan to GATT rules and disciplines and their earliest possible entry into GATT or its successor, the World Trade Organization (WTO). China's membership is crucial to effectively integrate China into the world economy and ensure the continuation of healthy market reforms in China.

Many in China hope that their country will join GATT by the end of this year, so that she can be a founding member of the WTO when it officially comes into being in 1995. Being a founding member is most important symbolically, confirming China's global status. It could also have practical consequences because it would allow China a role in establishing modes of operation and setting precedents, from the outset.

China's membership has been under discussion since a GATT working party on this subject was established in 1988. Discussions languished, however, both because of the Tiananmen tragedy and, more recently, the heavy attention paid in other capitals to completing the Uruguay Round. With the Round completed, it is now possible for Trilateral trade authorities to devote greater attention to China's admission. For the first time since 1989, the GATT working party resumed its efforts in March 1994.

There are two basic approaches to the China entry issue. One approach is to allow China to enter on easy terms, permitting GATT members to use normally GATT-illegal selective safeguards, targeted toward China, in the event of market disruptions. While some in China fear that this approach in the long-term would harm China by permitting continued violations of standard, most-favored-nation treatment, others regard it as the easiest and quickest form of entry, potentially protecting China against politically motivated sanctions. The other approach is the path most recently taken by Mexico in entering the GATT. As part of its accession agreement, Mexico agreed to a firm, phased-in program to achieve full GATT standards by a fixed time.

Because of their strong interest in maintaining the international trading system, the Trilateral countries should insist that China and Taiwan make firm commitments to meet GATT/WTO standards. The value to the Trilateral countries of having China and Taiwan in the GATT/WTO is precisely to secure their adherence to GATT principles and disciplines, and this is of great benefit to these economies as well. Acceptable tariff commitments, the dismantling of non-tariff barriers, transparency requirements, and adherence to GATT codes and disciplines (including those negotiated during the Uruguay Round) are all required for GATT admission. These requirements and dates for meeting them should be clearly spelled out in the accession agreements.

China's insistence that it be categorized as a "developing county" is another potential problem. This would allow China to maintain tariff protection for "infant industries," such as automobiles, machinery, and electronics. This will surely raise a cry from other GATT members, already frustrated by existing market access barriers in China. Under the GATT charter, such protective barriers remain in place for only three years and then extensions must be further negotiated. It is likely that both initial protections and later extensions will be contentious.

Despite these complexities, the Trilateral countries should work with China and Taiwan to assure their earliest possible membership in GATT/WTO consistent with the requirements of the international trade organizations. Both economies play an important role in the world economy, and therefore, each should be admitted as soon as it meets the requirements, without the accession of one dependent upon the other.

APEC

Efforts to deepen China's dialogue with its region are being carried out through the Asia-Pacific Economic Cooperation (APEC) forum. Although created only in 1989, APEC has already proved useful as a discussion forum, and it was given a further boost in November 1993 when an "informal leadership conference" occurred involving most of its then 15 members' top leaders, including China's Jiang Zemin. While many members emphasize that APEC is for consultation and is not a negotiating forum, it has begun to implement concrete suggestions for regional liberalization put forward by its working groups and "Eminent Persons Group." Because APEC has explicitly stated its intention to be a regional building block toward global economic liberalization, APEC can be a vehicle for assisting China's integration into the global economy.[6]

APEC is especially appealing because it has already successfully dealt with the thorny China membership problem. The People's Republic, Taiwan and Hong Kong were simultaneously admitted in 1991 and all three members participate in APEC meetings; but Taiwan and Hong Kong are represented at a lower governmental level than the PRC. This compromise has proved successful and could be a formula for other activities.

Encouraging China's integration through APEC also makes sense in that the Asia-Pacific region is so critical to China's economic development. In turn, China's sustained growth is a dynamo for the region. China's reform and open-door policies affect other Asia-Pacific countries, such as Indonesia and Vietnam, propelling them toward their own liberalization efforts.

MFN Status in the United States

The United States has insisted on tying China's continued most-favored-nation tariff treatment in the American market to its human rights performance. China has had conditional MFN status since 1979 under the Jackson-Vanik amendment to the 1974 Trade Act, which allowed such status for non-market economies that allowed or made progress in permitting free emigration. The continuation of this status requires annual Presidential approval, subject to Congressional veto.

The continuation of China's MFN status became controversial in the United States after the 1989 Tiananmen crackdown, with Congress almost vetoing former President Bush's annual extension. In June 1993, the Clinton Administration extended MFN treatment, but linked the 1994 extension to acceptable progress on human rights issues in the intervening year. The Administration hoped to restore a bipartisan approach to the China MFN issue, reestablish policy leadership in the Executive branch, give itself and the Chinese time to reassess the issue, and, hopefully, make substantive progress. But neither the Administration nor the Chinese followed up in a timely fashion, and the U.S. Administration faces the same issue in 1994 that it did in 1993.

Realistically, it is not politically possible for the Administration to renew MFN status without some continued linkage to China's human rights record. We recommend a one-year renewal in expectation that China will continue to make progress in its adherence to internationally accepted basic human rights. Not to renew would, in fact, be harmful to the cause of human rights in China. It would also entail enormous economic costs for China, the United States, and the economies most closely entwined in the trade between the two, such as Taiwan and Hong Kong. Finally, it would be damaging to U.S. relations with both Europe and Asia (which support an MFN approach to trade with China) and disruptive of the world trading system.

In the long-term, we hope that the United States will be able to extend MFN treatment to China without an annual review. The United States and all other countries have legitimate moral and political interests in human rights in other countries (see chapter VIII). But only the United States conditions MFN status on human rights considerations, and then only for certain Communist or formerly Communist countries. Furthermore, because of the political process surrounding the annual extensions, the U.S. standards are subjectively interpreted and may be changed by the

Congress or Executive. Ironically, many observers believe that China's human rights record is far better today than it was in 1979 when MFN was originally accorded and in the 1980s when it was annually extended without extensive controversy.

Europe, Japan, and Canada have no interest in the escalation of the tension between the United States and China on this matter, and they may be more effective in advancing human rights standards. Ongoing and firm dialogue with the Chinese at many levels on the issue of observance of international human rights standards to which China has agreed will be much more productive over time than unilateral threats to revoke MFN status.

VI. CHINA'S NATIONAL SECURITY

As stated in our introduction, China's leaders seek both military and economic power. For this reason, China's rise, if sustained and successful, presents a different challenge than the post-World War II reemergence of Japan and Germany as economic powers or of the Soviet Union as a military power. From a strategic perspective, three major questions arise from the military and security dimensions of China's emergence as a great power.

First, how will China use its growing military might? China is engaged in a significant military modernization program, supported by its booming economy. Its military budget is increasing, and sophisticated new weaponry is being imported from abroad, taking advantage of the cheap prices for defense hardware and technology on the world market, especially from Russia. At the same time, China's armed forces have been trimmed in an effort to increase their efficiency and professionalism. But the ultimate objectives of China's defense modernization are unclear.

Second, how will China's growing role as a supplier of military and dual-purpose technologies and equipment affect the international order? The most controversial of China's sales are to countries which are not committed to the international status quo and thus generally have more difficulty securing supplies from the Trilateral countries. This leads to questions about China's motives—are China's sales made with a political purpose in mind or are they purely commercial without consideration given to their geopolitical implications?

Finally, what positive contributions might China make to the reshaping of the international and regional order in the post-Cold War period? China has not been a major source of policy initiatives on the key security issues of the region, such as the North Korean nuclear threat. It appears to have a marked preference for bilateral consultations on security issues rather than action through multilateral institutions and processes. Might China develop a more constructive role as a security partner in multilateral settings with the Trilateral countries or its Asia-Pacific neighbors?

SECURITY NEEDS AND ASPIRATIONS

A Trilateral approach to China in the defense arena must be grounded in a realistic understanding of China's security needs and great power aspirations. As other countries, China's national security policy is rooted in perceived threats and goals. These perceived threats and goals are those of a great power. According to one Chinese strategist, Chinese leaders have three major security concerns: that Russia may reemerge as an expansionist power, that Japan may become remilitarized, and that the United States may become a hostile power. These are hypothetical threats in today's environment, but from a Chinese perspective, they are not terribly remote. Moreover, China's past humiliations at the hands of imperialist great powers are still deeply engrained in the minds of the Chinese political leaders and defense planners; to them this past experience justifies a continued and sustained effort to develop China's defense capabilities to a level needed to deter future threats. China's long-term aspiration, in the words of the same defense specialist referred to above, is that "China be truly accorded an equal status with other great powers."

This points to a central feature of China's national security policy—its reference points are other large powers. China does not want to be in an inferior position to other powers, but it currently perceives its forces to be manifestly inferior to those of the United States, a perception given urgency by the display of American strength in the Gulf War. For Chinese defense planners that war reconfirmed the validity of the direction of China's military modernization plotted in the Deng Xiaoping era, away from reliance on large mass forces and toward professionalism and the substitution of technology for manpower.

China's military modernization (or "catch-up") appears incongruous to many foreign observers in the post-Cold War environment. This environment would seem not to necessitate an increase in defense expenditures. Russia no longer constitutes an imminent threat, and its military capabilities, investments, and readiness are likely to continue to decline. Japan has also reduced its military expenditure from close to 1 percent of GNP to about 0.9 percent, and it continues to disavow any desire to have force projection capabilities. (It must be recognized, however, that from China's perspective, Japan is not an inconsiderable military power; in current exchange rate terms, Japan's military spending is much larger than China's.) Although the United States remains a global military superpower, U.S. defense personnel numbers, numbers of overseas military installations, and procurement levels have been substantially reduced. The U.S. level of defense expenditures as a percentage of GNP has dropped to the level of the late 1930s. In contrast to its presence in Europe, the United States has made only modest cutbacks in its forward presence in the Asia-Pacific region (the most significant was the termination of U.S. facilities in the Philippines), but the direction is clearly toward further reductions as security conditions permit.

China's continued defense build-up in this more benign environment obviously raises questions about China's intentions. China is a nuclear power. Other factors also call attention to Chinese ambitions. First, China continues to have territorial disputes with a number of its neighbors, including Russia, India, and a number of Southeast Asian countries whose claims in the South China Sea overlap its own. These neighbors are naturally suspicious that China aims at a superior military position to provide strong bargaining leverage with respect to its claims.

Second, since China's build-up is keyed on the major powers, it is impossible for smaller Asian states around China's border to maintain equivalent forces. These countries will be increasingly concerned about a less favorable relative balance. In this way, China's defense efforts could become the primary driving force of an Asian arms race. Some argue that this is already the case.

Third, Asian countries are deeply aware of China's propensity since the establishment of the People's Republic to use force in disputes with neighbors. Examples are its intervention in the Korean war in 1950-53, its efforts to oust Nationalist forces from Quemoy and Matsu islands in the mid-1950s, the Sino-Indian war of 1962, border incidents with Russia in 1969, its expulsion of South Vietnamese forces from the Paracels in 1974, its incursion into the northern reaches of Vietnam in 1979, and its clashes with Vietnamese forces in the Spratlys as recently as 1988. Whether or not China had justifiable reasons to use military force in these instances is not the issue here, nor is the cautious and limited nature of many of the Chinese interventions. The point is that China has demonstrated a will to use military force frequently in its relations with its neighbors and this very fact causes deep concern at a time when China is engaged in a visible modernization program. Furthermore, China has demonstrated an opportunistic willingness to forge close relations with and provide military assistance to North Korea, the Khmer Rouge, and Burma.

For the countries of Southeast Asia, China's policy toward the Spratlys in the South China Sea is regarded as a key test of China's goodwill toward the region. The issue is given added importance because of its energy-related implications. As noted in the previous chapter, China is becoming an oil importer, and will need perhaps 1 million barrels a day from the Middle East by the turn of the century.[1] As China's oil dependence grows, it has an increased stake in the Spratlys, which lie astride the sea routes leading north from the Malacca Straits. Moreover, the principal value of the islets lies in the shelf and sea resources associated with their 200-mile Exclusive Economic Zones. While specialists dispute the resource potential of the South China Sea, some believe the Spratlys area may have significant oil and gas deposits.

Two additional related features raise questions about China's military modernization: the lack of transparency about China's defense doctrines and the absence of tested political processes for assuring civilian control of the military. Unlike a growing number of other Asian countries, including Japan and South Korea, China does not publish an annual "white paper" on defense. And while all countries exercise secrecy in the area of national security, China practices an unusual degree of secrecy, obscuring or distorting basic defense information not only from foreigners but also from its own population. No procedure exists within the Chinese system comparable to U.S. Congressional hearings or parliamentary questioning in many Trilateral countries for eliciting public information on security doctrines or defense planning.

Internally, as noted in chapter III, Party or civilian control of the military is exercised only at the very top and the military has unfettered access to the Politburo. This naturally heightens concerns about the long-term capacity for civilian rulers to check and discipline the military and raises questions about the foreign policy roles and ambitions of the military. There are already signs of its assertiveness and independence on issues of foreign policy, especially in the case of the Spratlys and weapons sales.

CHINA'S ARMS SALES

Chinese frequently point out that their arms sales, although growing, are still far below those of the United States or the Trilateral world in general. Often, however, the buyers are involved in local arms races or appear to have aspirations that are disruptive of international order. China is a relatively new supplier whose sales are directed toward countries which for one reason or another confront difficulties in obtaining weapons from established arms suppliers. These tend to be developing countries—the list includes Algeria, Iran, Iraq, and Pakistan—seeking cheap weapons or access to more sophisticated technology denied to them by the Trilateral nations.

Thus, China's arms sales appear to be commercially motivated with little regard for their implications for international order. Last year's sale of M-11 surface-to-surface missile technology to Pakistan provides a case in point. The United States argued that the sale was in violation of the Missile Technology Control Regime (MTCR), an agreement which China has not signed but by which it agreed to abide. Therefore, under U.S. law, the Department of State had little choice but to apply sanctions. China argued that the M-11's range is less than the MTCR minimum of 300 kilometers, and it branded the U.S. sanctions as "a naked hegemonic act" that "has brutally violated the basic norms governing international relations."[2] Behind the more technical arguments lay U.S. concerns that the missiles would contribute to the South Asian arms race—an area where the two major powers, India and Pakistan, have nuclear weapons capabilities. The United States also felt rebuffed in its efforts to discuss the missile sale at an earlier stage with the Chinese.

China decries what it regards, somewhat legitimately, as a double standard. Chinese commentators have noted that the West sells to developing countries advanced aircraft with the same or better capabilities as M-11 missiles. Moreover, it notes that the MTCR was negotiated by the Western nations without Chinese participation and that the 300-kilometer limit was established with Western missile characteristics in mind.

CHINA'S CONTRIBUTIONS TO INTERNATIONAL ORDER

China's leaders avow that at a time when China's highest priority is to concentrate on its own economic modernization, its foreign policy is animated above all by the desire for a stable environment. China has, particularly since the end of the Cold War, improved its relations with a number of neighbors, including Russia, South Korea, Vietnam, and India. It used its influence with its long-time clients, the Khmer Rouge, to encourage them to engage in the Cambodian peace process, and it contributed 426 observers and engineers to the UN peacekeeping mission in Cambodia. It appears to have encouraged

North Korea to submit to international inspections of its nuclear facilities, while counselling the international community to use diplomacy rather than economic sanctions to reach an acceptable inspection accord with the North. It has joined the ASEAN Regional Forum, an intergovernmental Asia-Pacific security dialogue scheduled to hold its first ministerial-level consultation this year. Beyond its immediate region, China did not use its veto in the UN Security Council to oppose multilateral intervention to restore Kuwait's sovereignty following the Iraqi invasion.

Thus, while China has cooperated with other countries on regional and global security issues, it has not been in the forefront of multilateral regional or global efforts. Indeed, China often appears to be a somewhat reluctant follower, using the possibility of noncooperation as a lever to maximize its influence. It seems to prefer bilateral rather than multilateral means of interacting with other countries on politico-security issues. Where opportunities exist to en hance China's influence, it is ready to exploit them. A recent example is China's efforts to exploit Myanmar's (Burma's) isolation and desperation to mount a major assistance effort and strengthen its position in that country. On a variety of issues from arms control to North Korea, it has shown relatively little interest in working intensively with other countries on a common agenda, raising doubts about its ultimate intentions.

The doubts about China's commitment to regional and global peace and security will continue in the absence of a strong, more visible Chinese role in protecting the international order. As an emerging power, and one emerging at a time of fundamental change in the structure of international politics, China has a responsibility to clarify its commitment to a stable international order, not simply through its rhetoric but through its foreign policy behavior and activity in international organizations.

POLICY IMPLICATIONS FOR TRILATERAL COUNTRIES

The Trilateral countries should emphasize their desire to treat China as a security partner in the pursuit of common security concerns. The main elements of this security partnership are the following:

1) The Trilateral countries should respect the legitimate security concerns of China and not seek to undermine China's security position. Reciprocally, they expect China to be sensitive to the legitimate security concerns of the Trilateral countries and their friends and allies.

2) The Trilateral countries should seek to maintain official and non-official bilateral, regional, and global dialogues with the Chinese on security issues. Through such dialogues, the Trilateral countries should state their own security interests clearly. These interests include the unity and economic vitality of China. They also include the integrity and economic well-being of the smaller countries around China, such as Vietnam.

3) As a security partner, China should be expected to increase the transparency of its defense efforts and to contribute to confidence-building measures—to improve understanding of its security interests and reassure other countries about its defensive posture. Transparency requires the disclosure and exchange of information on such matters as defense doctrines, defense planning, procurements, spending levels, exercises, and external military ties. Confidence-building measures can include prior notification and observation of maneuvers or exercises, joint exercises, ship visits, mutual inspections, and measures to avoid incidents. The Trilateral countries welcome China's participation in such measures on a bilateral, regional, and global basis.

4) The Trilateral countries desire China to be a full partner in the development of subregional, regional and global regimes in such areas as non-proliferation, chemical and biological weapons, missile technology control, and further strategic arms limitations and reductions.

5) The Trilateral countries should welcome China's full participation in specific areas of common concern (but not necessarily identical interests), including the North Korean nuclear weapons issue and preventing arms races in South and Southeast Asia. The ASEAN Regional Forum provides one avenue for such discussions, although this process is in a very early stage of development and is too broad to deal effectively with some subregional issues.

6) The Trilateral countries should welcome China's broader participation in United Nations peacekeeping efforts, and engage China more actively in discussions of regional peace and security issues beyond those in Asia. These include issues in the Middle East and Africa.

7) The Trilateral countries should point out that they seek to contribute to a stable international political environment, which, as

China's leaders have acknowledged, is of benefit to China. In this regard, the United States intends to maintain its military strength in the Asia-Pacific region, and Japan intends to continue its basic "defensive defense" approach to national security. Japan's approach requires its continued alliance with the United States.

8) Where the Trilateral countries have concerns about China's defense and arms transfer policies, these should be made as clear as possible. The Trilateral countries should not hesitate to use their considerable economic leverage with China where China has clearly violated international understandings or has engaged in behavior that undermines peace and stability. China should understand that its behavior will affect aid flows and access to credits and technology.

9) This chapter has made fewer references to Europe than to other Trilateral areas, but Europe's roles in the engagement of China on security issues are nevertheless substantial. Britain and France sit with China as permanent members of the United Nations Security Council, a key framework for China's engagement on security matters of global concern. A variety of security regimes of global import include (or should include) both Europe and China. Active European countries in these regimes can in some ways articulate the broader international interest to China more clearly than the United States and Japan, whose security involvements with China are more immediate. And yet Europe has substantial direct interests as well. Europe shares China's concern about the potential reemergence of an expansionist Russia, and the search for a mutually beneficial relationship with the new Russia will need to include China. Furthermore, as the economic stakes of European countries in East Asia continue to increase, Europe's stake in the political stability and progress of the area will increase as well. Europe's rapidly growing trade with East Asia surpassed trade with the United States in 1992.

VII. Global Issues and China's Role

OVERVIEW

Issues such as nuclear non-proliferation, environmental degradation, population control and public health affect nations from all regions of the world and at all levels of development. When the Chernobyl nuclear power plant had a meltdown in Ukraine, a radioactive cloud reached the westernmost tip of Europe. CFC chemicals emitted in the United States relate to ozone depletion which is affecting the food chain in the seas around Antarctica. A sexually transmitted disease originating in West Africa has become the scourge of urban America, Europe and Southeast Asia. The global community has begun to recognize that the only way to combat such problems is by working together.

Cold War bipolarity no longer paralyzes and politicizes global efforts. Western Europe and the United States are now providing aid to Ukraine to reencase the melted reactor at Chernobyl. New global treaties, such as the Biodiversity Treaty, have emerged.

It is clear that China's engagement in these efforts is crucial. Not only does China constitute more than twenty percent of the world's population, but her rapid economic growth and emerging global status involve her more deeply in these global problems, and make her more able to help in their solution.

There are reasons to hope that China will be an active participant in international cooperative efforts. China is eager to gain international recognition of her heightened status, and recognizes that participation in global initiatives is a sure way to gain prestige and respect. She has already signalled a willingness to cooperate on certain issues. Indeed, on some environmental issues she is on a par with or ahead of some of the major industrialized nations. She was one of the early ratifiers of the Biodiversity Treaty, a treaty the United States has still not ratified.[1] She agreed to adhere to the ban on dumping radioactive waste at sea at the same time as Great Britain.[2] Even in negotiations where China still holds serious objections, such as the current discussions on regulating the trade in tropical timber, she has found herself in the company of the European Union and Austria.[3]

Yet, there is still much room for improvement, and good reason for concern. Involving China in multilateral efforts is a particularly sensitive endeavor, due to China's conception of herself and her place in the world. While she is gaining increasing experience with it, China is still not comfortable with multilateral action. For China, relations with other countries have tended to be bilateral, and saturated with traditional power politics. Because of this *realpolitik* lens, Beijing views international commitments that could interfere with China's short-term growth as an attempt to "keep China down," especially when she believes that other major powers are not adhering to these same commitments. The international community will have to work closely with China to convince her that participating in multilateral cooperative efforts can be to China's long-term advantage, and that China will not be the only country actually abiding by new laws and regulations.

A second hurdle will be China's current obsession with economic development above all else. Many of the problems that require global attention are exacerbated by nations which focus only on immediate economic gain. The most obvious examples are pollution and proliferation. International norms that might hamper China's economic ambitions are likely to be rejected. Furthermore, China often lacks the capital, technology and knowledge necessary to make the expensive changes required by international regulations. Without assistance, China may be incapable of adhering to new international norms.

Even when China is willing, she for the most part lacks the laws and institutions to enforce international laws. This has been a great source of frustration to her trading partners, and is sure to be a similar obstacle in solving global issues.

NON-PROLIFERATION

Perhaps the most pressing global issue in the post-Cold War era is the proliferation of weapons of mass destruction. In the wake of the fall of the Soviet Union, a large arsenal of highly destructive weapons and technology has been left in the hands of cash-strapped states. Much of it is now being sold in unstable regions of the world, potentially triggering greater instability and regional arms build-ups. China has bought fighter jets and missiles from Russia. As China reemerges as a global power, she believes she must have the defense capabilities of such a power.

On the export side, China's People's Liberation Army has become actively involved in the arms trade, eager to gain hard currency for its modernization drive. We have already noted the questionable sale of missile technology to Pakistan. China has continued to resist fully cooperating with any arms export control regimes, and has used her position on the UN Security Council to block plans to set up an information exchange on arms exports. China often feels that such efforts are designed to keep China down, while letting the other established powers go about their business as usual. She is surely confirmed in her views by the active arms trade carried on by the major powers in the West.

However, China does not wish to be isolated from the world community. She deeply resents being categorized as a "rogue state," along with such countries as Iran, Iraq and Burma. Such designations by U.S. National Security Advisor Anthony Lake and Ambassador to the UN Madeleine Albright deeply wound China's pride.[4] China is participating in some international cooperative efforts to control proliferation, and would like this to be acknowledged. On March 16, 1994, President Clinton extended the U.S. moratorium on nuclear testing through September 1995, deepening the division between China and other nuclear powers which have chosen to refrain from testing. This should ultimately put additional pressure on China to comply with the international test ban as she seeks to diminish her renegade reputation.

China has agreed to abide by the Missile Technology Control Regime, although she has yet to become a signatory. Allowing China a fuller say in the determination of the MTCR may further motivate China to abide by its rules. China's engagement in the international effort to prevent North Korea from going nuclear is another example of China's willingness to participate in international non-proliferation activities (see chapter VI).

In sum, China's record on global non-proliferation efforts has been mixed. The combination of China's paranoia and the West's hypocrisy have worked against China becoming an effective member of global non-proliferation efforts.

ENVIRONMENTAL ISSUES

China suffers from particularly bad air pollution because of her almost exclusive dependence on coal for her increasing energy demands. High-sulfur-content coal provides almost three-quarters of the country's energy, and the sulfur in the coal leads to acid rain. China is believed to be the top acid rain producer in its region, causing destruction of forests in far-off Siberia, Korea and Japan.[5]

Irresponsible industrialization has caused massive water pollution. More than two-thirds of household and industrial waste water is dumped untreated into rivers, lakes and the sea. Approximately 30 percent of China's population does not have access to a safe and clean source of water. There is a correspondingly high incidence of diarrhea and other intestinal diseases that commonly accompany polluted water supplies.[6] China's policies are causing damage to the nation's production as well as its health: shortages of clean water and clean air are lowering agricultural yields and pushing up manufacturing costs.

China's irresponsible water resource management and air pollution have already begun to affect neighboring countries and the global environment. Coastal pollution is increasing all along the East and South China Seas, and the pollution is sure to hit the fishing industry in the near future. China's emissions of greenhouse gases, particularly carbon-dioxide, are a significant portion of global emissions.

In response, there have been increasing attempts in the region and in the wider international sphere to help China improve its ecological practices. China and Japan agreed in December 1993 to an environmental protection treaty, following the treaties China has already signed with South Korea, India and Canada. The China-Japan agreement is a particularly important signal of progress, as China admitted for the first time in a treaty draft to the existence of acid rain and air pollution in China.[7] China has also begun its own domestic initiatives to curtail pollution. Beijing has plans to build a huge hydroelectric project in the Three Gorges area of the Yangtze River, which, though it will create major environmental challenges of its own, will provide energy for the region without producing carbon-dioxide. China has been praised for its efforts to control energy consumption and promote industrial efficiency.[8]

However, many of the environmental rules and regulations Beijing has instituted have run up against cadre corruption and weak laws and institutions. Tougher penalties might jeopardize economic growth and jobs, something the central government isn't willing to consider. The government's priorities were made clear by an official at China's national Environmental Protection Agency: "We must simply try to slow down the rate of increase of pollution as China develops—but we cannot stop the development."[9] It will take a full-scale international effort, combined with significant incentives and technological cooperation, to steer China towards more environmentally responsible development policies.

HEALTH AND POPULATION POLICIES

In addition to the health issues connected to environmental degradation, China will be increasingly asked to participate in global attempts to control the spread of highly infectious diseases. While AIDS is still virtually non-existent in China, its rapid spread throughout Southeast Asia guarantees that HIV will eventually hit China.[10] Certain areas of China with a preexisting high incidence of sexually transmitted diseases, such as Yunnan province, are likely to be the first to experience the AIDS scourge. International efforts (primarily through the World Health Organization) which focus on prevention, and integrating AIDS education into general sex education programs, could be of great utility in China. While the Communist Party might find such programs distasteful to its prudish consciousness, there are powerful arguments for taking action now to slow the spread of AIDS in China.[11]

How China handles this disease will be interesting, given how it has handled matters of family planning thus far. Its coercive tactics to control population growth, while widely condemned in the international community, have been effective. Nevertheless, China's population is still growing, and is projected to approach 1.3 billion people by the year 2000.[12] It is unclear how well the central government will be able to maintain control over such a fundamental decision as how large a family to have, particularly if predicted political liberalization does ensue.

China's huge population poses a serious challenge to China's domestic stability and the welfare of China's neighbors. As noted earlier, there is already massive internal migration in China, as more and more poor farmers from China's agricultural interior migrate to the booming coastal urban centers. Beijing has sought to regulate this migration, but loosened travel restrictions enacted as part of economic reform ensure that more of China will be on the move.

Emigration from China has also caused regional and international concern, especially the illegal smuggling of Chinese migrants into other countries. The boatload of smuggled Chinese migrants who arrived on the U.S. West Coast and were passed off to Mexico was an embarrassment to all the governments involved. It is certainly in China's and the international interest to curtail such smuggling, and help China with her population concerns. Over the long term, helping ensure the success of China's economic growth is the best way to help avoid a mass exodus of Chinese, which would surely overwhelm the world. As it is, if 0.1 percent of China's population decided to emigrate, it would mean the release of 1.2 million more persons in a world already awash in migrants.

POLICY IMPLICATIONS

It is urgent that the Trilateral nations do their utmost to include China in efforts to attack these various global problems. They must be very careful to make it clear to China that her involvement will be to her own benefit. They must communicate that these efforts are not intended to stunt China's growth, but to make her growth more sustainable. As part of this, the Trilateral nations should admit that they also have room for improvement in the areas in which they are criticizing China.

The primary focus should be on non-proliferation concerns, as China's activities in this sphere have been most troubling, and her activities could upset the security balance in several already unstable regions. The key factor will be working with China, rather than trying unilaterally to force her to conform to international rules. It will be crucial to build trust between China and the Trilateral nations, so that attempts to curtail her arms exports will not be seen by China as an attempt to edge her out of lucrative arms markets. Furthermore, making sure that China has a say in the shape of control regimes will be crucial to ensure her full involvement (witness her complaints about the MTCR because she had no say in determining its parameters). China should be part of efforts to extend the current moratorium on nuclear testing.

The Trilateral nations should be careful not to be hypocritical in their demands on China. While Trilateral countries have a right to be concerned about the rapid rise in China's production of carbon-dioxide, China's production of CO_2 is still less than half that of the United States.[13]

The world community must behave consistently and logically towards China on global issues. These are areas where a lockstep approach among Trilateral countries is preferable. If one nation "cuts a deal" with China, for instance for sales of either weapons or environmentally destructive chemicals, it will critically undermine international efforts. Foreign aid to China should be guided by international standards, and perhaps a new framework should be developed to ensure a consistent approach that is constructive for China and the world community.

Certain guidelines have been set up for Japan's Official Development Assistance (ODA) that could be productively applied to the aid programs of other OECD countries as well. The new Japanese

ODA "charter" makes aid contingent on three prerequisites which directly apply to China: control of military expenditures and of weapons acquisition and sales, progress on human rights and democratization, and concern for environmental issues. While Japan has been very cautious in applying these new guidelines (it is highly unlikely that Japan will suddenly cut off its ODA to China), it has promised to become tougher in the future on ODA recipients who do not show progress in these areas.[14] We recommend instituting similar guidelines for all Trilateral aid, rather than further unilateral initiatives.

Indeed, China is in desperate need of funds for environmental clean-up and the acquisition of ecologically sound technologies. We encourage all Trilateral nations to boost their aid for such purposes, particularly focusing on the subsidization of clean coal technologies and less-polluting energy sources. International information exchanges should also be promoted. Learning tours (such as that taken by a delegation of Chinese experts to examine Canada's work on reducing greenhouse gas emissions) are of inestimable worth, both in passing on technical knowledge and in improving international ties.[15]

Trilateral nations should look upon China as a budding market for their new environmental technologies, thus encouraging trade and helping China tackle her environmental problems simultaneously. This will require certain Trilateral countries to overcome their unconstructive ideological barriers which have prevented China from getting such aid in the past. An example is the United States withholding funds from China in its U.S.-Asian Environmental Partnership program to protest of China's population control methods. As discussed before, a bullying approach is sure to backfire when applied to China, but assisting her with aid and advice may produce some positive results.

Finally, cooperating with China in programs at the UN, World Bank, IAEA, and other international organizations could be very helpful in training and educating China's professionals and technocrats. Such activities help create a more internationally oriented atmosphere in the government, which would allow these newly trained individuals to be more vocal. In fields from global warming to international banking, there is emerging an increasing number of technocrats from the younger generation who hold a much more interdependent world view than their predecessors.

VIII. The Effective and Good Governance of China

The Trilateral countries have an interest in the effective and good governance of China. All of the foreign and domestic policies that the outside world seeks from China—a well-regulated market economy; steady growth; weapons development, acquisitions, and sales that contribute to international and regional stability; proper attention to environmental issues; humane family-planning programs; improvement in the well-being of the populace—can only be attained if the Chinese government is capable of carrying out its international obligations and implementing its regulations. Such a government must elicit the respect of the Chinese people. Nepotism, corruption, inflation, capital flight, and bureaucratic slothfulness erode the effectiveness of the government and contribute to popular scorn for its leaders. In contrast, a benevolent government that responds to popular demands and that provides opportunities to the populace to participate in their governance enhances its legitimacy and is more likely to be stable.

Each people on earth will judge its rulers in light of its own experiences and traditions. Thus, to many Americans, a good government is one which allows its citizens relatively unfettered access to pistols, rifles and shotguns, while in most other nations, the deaths resulting from this weaponry would be taken as a sure sign of governmental incompetence. To most Asians, a society in which the family is in decay and divorce rates are high is not providing for basic human rights of children to be nurtured as moral beings. We must begin discussion of good governance in China by asking: How do Chinese think about the task of governance?

THE CONFUCIAN HERITAGE AND THE PURPOSES OF GOVERNMENT

We noted in Chapter II that the cultural traditions of China are more rich and varied than many imagine. Confucian pragmatism, Daoist mysticism, hedonistic folk religions, and Buddhist aestheticism coexist even within the same individuals. Yet certain powerful tendencies in thought and practice traceable to Confucius and his disciples are widespread, both in popular culture and among the sophisticated intelligentsia.

The Western liberal tradition considers each individual to possess a unique combination of qualities, which give that individual his or her distinctive identity. In contrast, the dominant Chinese tradition asserts that human identity is derived from the network of social relations in which one is inevitably enmeshed.[1] Thus, one's sense of being stems not from innate qualities but from one's place in society and from the thoughts one's parents, siblings, spouse, community, and polity have cultivated in one's mind. Human beings, according to this view, do not have innate characteristics; they are malleable. And happiness is achieved not through discovery of the self and development of one's individuality and innate talents but through proper performance of social obligations.

These contrasting views produce divergent notions about the purposes of government. In the Western liberal tradition, the individual, touched by grace and endowed with inalienable rights, is paramount. Good government must protect the individual and human rights from the machinations of fellow beings—especially from the misrule of leaders. In the Confucian tradition, the community is paramount, for only through a virtuous community can individuals achieve their potential. According to this view, the primary purpose of good government is to create a harmonious social order within which individuals are able to perform their social roles and responsibilities.

Thus, the landmark documents on governance in the Western liberal tradition—the English Magna Carta, the American Declaration of Independence and Gettysburg Address, the French Declaration of the Rights of Man—emphasize strictures upon rulers and attach primacy to liberty. The key task in framing a constitution is to protect the ruled from abuse of power by the rulers. In China until recent times, the key task, in contrast, was to forge institutions that would yield virtuous rulers and would grant these leaders unfettered access to their subjects, in order to foster moral communities. In the Confucian lexicon, filial piety, loyalty, ritual or propriety were among the most esteemed virtues, while the concepts of individualism (*geren zhuyi*) and human rights (*ren quan*) were introduced into the language in the 19th century.

We have purposefully exaggerated the contrast between Western liberal thought and the dominant strands of Confucianism. In fact, many Western political theorists have voiced ideas that bear considerable resemblance to prevalent Chinese views, and some of the diverse intellectual traditions within Confucianism are congruent with Western liberal and even democratic thought.[2]

Nor does our contrast of Western liberal and traditional Confucian thought imply that Chinese are more prepared to accept gross abuses of human dignity than Westerners are. Certain universal standards of human conduct transcend differences among cultures, and Chinese theories of governance place at least as much emphasis upon benevolent and humane rule as Western theories do. Further, Western ideas of governance have had a tremendous impact on China in the past century. People as diverse as John Dewey and Karl Marx, as well as the social gospel of missionaries, have left their legacy in contemporary Chinese views of governance. Deng and his advisors have been quite eclectic in their deliberate borrowing from East Asia, the former Communist states, and the developed democracies.

Our purpose has been a more limited one: China's rise represents the rise of a distinctive yet complex civilization. Its leaders, products of their culture, approach their tasks of rule with their own understandings about the nature of human beings and the purposes of governance. These understandings are different from those of the Trilateral countries. It is therefore unreasonable to expect China to be governed in the same fashion as Japan, North America, or Western Europe. Chinese political traditions do not neglect the importance of the individual, but they place more emphasis on cultivation of the individual in a social context. It is important for the leaders of Trilateral countries to approach China with a sense of respect and understanding of its political traditions, rather than disdaining and seeking to transform those traditions to accord with Western values.

While the international community has a legitimate interest in the peaceful evolution of the Chinese political system (an interest China fully shares), many current Chinese leaders have felt that much of the international pressure on her has been a condescending attempt to reshape China in a Western image. They have argued that the Chinese people must find their own path of political development, dictated by their own cultural heritage and developmental requirements rather than by foreign standards. Many in the international community basically agree with this argument, and feel that continued economic development, opening to the outside world, and involvement in the international community will necessitate a more open, tolerant political system. But there are also actions the outside world can take to assist this process.

THE POLITICAL RAMIFICATIONS OF
ECONOMIC LIBERALIZATION

Many examples, including those of South Korea and Taiwan, suggest that economic development eventually will lead to political liberalization. Deng Xiaoping and his reformers, while certainly not intentionally, are establishing the basis for a more open polity: they are creating a strong middle class that will be willing to become politically engaged and will demand the opportunity to influence public policy.

The increased occupational diversity of Chinese society is also bringing about political change. Economic growth is turning some parts of Chinese society into winners: farmers who have benefited from land reform, and private entrepreneurs in the booming coastal regions. It is simultaneously threatening to turn others into losers: those employed at economically unviable state enterprises. The influence of these vying interests is already evident as the government vacillates between their conflicting demands. Eventually, the diversification of interests in society will have to be expressed within the government itself. The demands will become too varied, and the protesters too numerous. At that time, the government will have to create institutional outlets for these varied and numerous societal demands.

There is already general recognition in Beijing that political reform must eventually follow economic reform. CCP General Secretary Zhao Ziyang's seven-point political reform program, presented at the 13th Party Congress in 1987, reflected this awareness. While the Tiananmen crackdown temporarily derailed these processes, Communist Party reform efforts have been renewed. Beijing's not-so-secret formula for political renewal may be reminiscent of the suggestions put forth by Bao Tong, Zhao Ziyang's advisor. It is likely that in the near future the Party will loosen some of its control over society, allowing for more pluralistic dialogue, while still making clear that all changes must take place within the confines of Communist one-party rule.[3]

While these future reforms may seem minor compared to the rapid democratization that has occurred in Eastern Europe and the former Soviet Union, most Chinese fear the chaos that could accompany rapid political change. China is much more drawn to the models of economic and political liberalization in her region, and has already modeled elements of her development on Asian countries which share China's Confucian culture—Taiwan, Japan, Korea and Singapore.

RECENT TRAUMAS AND POLITICAL REFORM

China's own recent traumatic history offers yet another reason for believing Beijing is likely to change. The upheaval of the later Mao years, which culminated in the massive social destruction of the Cultural Revolution, has left an indelible mark on the Chinese people. It left all levels of Chinese society seriously disillusioned with the Party and its ideology. This condition motivated Deng Xiaoping's reforms—Deng recognized that this time the Party had to deliver a better life.

A similar responsiveness to changing attitudes among lower-level officials and the populace could very well encourage Deng's successors to accelerate the process of political reform. Torture; detention of prisoners without notification of family; widespread and somewhat arbitrary use of the death penalty; government oppression of venerated religious traditions among both Han and ethnic minorities; callous, inhumane, and unpunished enforcement by local officials of family-planning regulations; corruption; nepotism; and harsh prison conditions are all practices that engender a cynical attitude among the populace toward their rulers and detract from the support the rulers obtain for the economic gains their programs have generated. Partly because of universal notions about human dignity, partly because many of these practices offend deeply ingrained Chinese standards of conduct, and partly because Western notions of human rights are influencing thinking among both the leaders and influential strata of society, Deng's successors are likely to face increasing pressures and incentives to diminish the harsh and oppressive features of Communist rule.

Further, signs already exist that the next generation of rulers is likely to seek institutional remedies to the problems of corruption, nepotism, and the widespread and arbitrary abuse of power. The underlying problem, of course, is the lack of a legal system, the absence of an independent judiciary, and a coercive apparatus—the police and army—that is not under effective civilian control. The army and police are responsive to commands of individual rulers, and are not under the discipline of law. This situation not only facilitates the abuse of power but inhibits the development of a well-regulated, predictable market economy.

The solution, supported by Chinese, international, and Western liberal notions, must be found in several political reforms: the development of a legal system and independent judiciary; the invigoration of parliamentary bodies at various levels to monitor the behavior of bureaucrats; the enhancement of civilian control over the police and military; and greater freedom for the media so investigative journalists can report on abuse of power. These reforms are not an imposition of alien Western notions upon resistant Chinese. In fact, measures in all four of these areas—some timid, some bold—have been launched in the Deng era. These institutional reforms are contentious and challenge strong vested interests, but they enjoy strong constituencies of support as well. The debates have centered on how best to carry out these political reforms—in what sequence, how fast, and at what risk.

POLICY IMPLICATIONS FOR TRILATERAL COUNTRIES

Recognizing the opportunity to encourage political reform in China, but also the unconstructive nature of some present Trilateral methods of forcing such change, there are three main policy directions which we recommend: (1) The Trilateral countries at most should establish only loose linkages between the Chinese human rights record and their own trade policies; human rights performance should not be a precondition for maintaining or expanding commercial relations. (2) The Trilateral nations should help China carry out political reforms through international institutions and NGOs. (3) The international community should quietly encourage the Chinese government to pay particular attention to the yearnings of its ethnic minorities.

Human Rights and Trade
We believe that improvements in human rights should not be made a precondition for maintaining or expanding normal commercial relations with China. The precondition implies that the two objectives are antithetical, whereas in fact they are mutually supportive. Expanded trade necessitates the development of a legal system; contact with the outside world awakens new aspirations for freedom. China's new entrepreneurial classes would be harmed by external strictures on trade. Preconditions, such as those the United States has

applied, arouse Chinese nationalism. And even if these preconditions are met, the measures demanded would not fundamentally alter China's human rights condition. The long-term solution, which both Chinese and the Trilateral countries recognize, is in the area of institution-building: strengthening the legal system, expanding the roles of parliaments, enhancing the authority of the courts, strengthening civilian control of the military and police, and fostering a free press. Here is where the Trilateral countries, in cooperation with the Chinese, should place their emphasis.

International Organizations and NGOs

The United States should move from a unilateral to a multilateral framework to discuss good governance with China. This will make it easier for Beijing to respond to foreign requests, as these responses will not be seen by China as caving in to another power. As discussed, China has her own reasons for wanting to improve her political environment, and she is equally concerned about becoming internationally isolated because of her domestic policies. A coordinated, multilateral approach could achieve greater results than the unilateral approach.

Recognition that China will find its own way to political openness does not excuse it from an obligation to guarantee internationally recognized human rights as defined in the 1948 UN Universal Declaration of Human Rights and widely accepted declarations and collateral documents. Our countries should emphasize that China's position on the UN Security Council entails responsibilities as well as rewards. It must be made clear to China that if she wishes to be a global power, she must develop a legitimate legal system, and institute civil protections worthy of a great and stable nation.

China's turnabout on access to prisoners is clearly part of China's strategy to improve her international standing, improve human rights conditions, and avoid seeming to have caved in to Western pressure. By granting the International Committee of the Red Cross, an international NGO, access to Chinese prisons, China does not feel that her sovereign authority is being violated by another nation. It is also helpful that the Red Cross reports are confidential, and are only to be seen in Beijing.⁴ While it is possible that these moves by Beijing were yet another cynical move to ensure renewed MFN status, it is worth noting that when China chose to make a move forward on human rights, it was an NGO that she embraced.

Minority Rights

The treatment of minorities and Tibet must be addressed in any discussion of effective and good governance in China.[5] This is both a simple issue and an extremely complex issue that is difficult to address in limited space. In simple terms, Han rule of China's ethnic minorities has been oppressive. Religious traditions have not been respected. Cultural heritages have been destroyed. The talents of indigenous peoples have not been developed so that they can assume ever greater responsibilities in leading their areas. Put simply, this is misrule on a vast scale.

Put in more complex terms, however, the relations between the Han Chinese and the minorities involve ambiguous histories, ill-defined borders, and relations between people of different occupations and civilizations.

For example, in the case of Tibet, the spiritual and political leaders of the Buddhist theocracy—the Dalai Lama and the Panchen Lama—historically enjoyed considerable autonomy within their territorially ill-defined area. From their perspective, they were sovereign in their domain, but they also paid obeisance to the distant Chinese emperor. They requested the emperor to dispatch forces on several occasions to settle disputes in Tibet. In the Qing dynasty (1644-1911), several emperors were adherents of the Dalai Lama, and hence recognized his spiritual authority. The Imperial Court patronized Tibetan Buddhist temples. But at the same time, leaders of the Tibetan theocracy, with other Inner Asian rulers, resided in Chengde, the imperial summer residence north of Beijing. There, the Tibetans and other Inner Asian rulers participated in the rituals that symbolized their subordination to the Chinese emperor. Thus, the situation for several centuries was highly ambiguous, and history therefore supports both the claims of those who wish to assert that Tibet was independent and those who claim that it was part of the Chinese empire.

Territorially, too, the issue of Tibet is complicated. Less than two million Tibetans reside in the region defined by the Chinese government today as Tibet. Approximately nine million Tibetans today reside in a vast area that includes substantial portions of today's Sichuan, Gansu and Qinghai provinces. They are interspersed among Han, Mongol, and various Islamic peoples and actually are a minority within this greater area. Yet, this entire area is claimed by those promoting Tibetan independence.

The Tibetans have been a nomadic, upland people practicing a highly elaborate and rich form of Buddhism. The Han Chinese are a sedentary, lowland people, with different religious beliefs. As is tragically the case for many of the world's nomadic peoples, the Tibetans have suffered from brutality and the destruction of their civilization. The situation has been aggravated by several factors, including Tibet's geostrategic importance to Beijing and recent large-scale Han Chinese immigration into Tibet (and the social consequences which have ensued). Chinese attempts to define an autonomous sphere of responsibilities for the Tibetans have floundered upon different views of what is religious and appropriately under minority jurisdiction and what is secular and subject to central government direction.

In discussions of Tibetans and other minority groups in Xinjiang, the Trilateral nations must take these complexities into account. They should encourage dramatic improvements in Chinese rule in Tibet and elsewhere, and should support negotiations between the Dalai Lama and the authorities in Beijing. Trilateral countries should be prepared to extend development assistance to the provincial government and residents of Tibet through international agencies such as the World Bank and ADB, to improve the quality of education, hospitals, agricultural and pastoral practices, and so on. But they should not arouse expectations of external support that they are not prepared to meet.

IX. Summary of Policy Recommendations

OVERVIEW

The international community is faced with a test. Its response to China's emergence as a global power will signal whether the international community can successfully operate within the framework of multilateral, cooperative action. The Trilateral nations must engage, not contain China. Cooperative, multilateral action is the best way to engage China. Both China and the Trilateral nations must work together to build sustainable, rather than astronomical growth in China. There must be cooperation in building institutions within China, and on the regional and global level, to channel growth and resolve differences. But the Trilateral countries must also recognize that a cooperative approach may not elicit a constructive Chinese response. And in any case, the strength and prosperity of the Trilateral countries—not their weakness—generate Chinese respect. Such classic considerations as balance of power, realism, and a keen sense of the Trilateral interests must also govern Western and Japanese thinking about China.

Our recommendations apply to the global, regional and sub-regional levels. The international community should build on the existing integrative frameworks in Asia, such as APEC and the ASEAN Regional Forum, which greatly enhance China's regional interdependence without setting up barriers against outsiders. It is critical that China establish firm and lasting ties in Asia, which will ensure a stable and prosperous environment for the whole region.

Regional multilateral organizations can greatly contribute to global integration. APEC was a constant advocate for a successfully concluded Uruguay Round, and adopted measures for market liberalization designed to spur the GATT negotiations. Regional organizations can also provide useful models for broader international organizations: the membership compromise worked out for the three parts of China in APEC could be relevant for GATT.

Our recommended policy on China requires engaging China in regional and global problem-solving in several areas: economic integration, security matters, global issues, and international human rights standards. On economic issues, the most pressing concern is getting China into the World Trade Organization. The combination of China's increasingly significant impact on the world economy with the insufficiently regulated nature of her economic growth could destabilize the international economy. China must be brought into the fold of the WTO, which can help China build the institutions necessary to monitor her growth, and which will ensure that China abides by international trade and investment rules.

Establishing China's place in a global and regional security framework is equally critical. Without a stable security environment, China's growth, and her relations with her economic partners, are sure to be warped. The third area, global issues, is likewise crucial, as there is little point in discussing the world's future if the international community cannot cooperate to reduce the likelihood of world destruction. It is an absolute imperative that China work with her neighbors and global partners to improve global environmental practices and population policies, to control trade in weapons of mass destruction, and to control trafficking in illicit drugs. A fourth concern involves the future of Hong Kong and Taiwan. The fifth aspect, good governance, requires great sensitivity and imagination on the part of the Trilateral countries and China. While China may be justified in feeling unfairly singled out on this issue, it is also fair to say that China must address the issue of political reform. Economic liberalization creates pressures for political opening, and it is in China's interest to see the successful progression of both movements. The Trilateral nations should generously assist Chinese efforts to build the wide range of institutions that would contribute to good and effective governance.

ECONOMIC INTEGRATION

1. Encourage China to Become Member of GATT/WTO as Rapidly as Possible by Agreeing to GATT Rules

The Trilateral countries have an important stake in assuring the commitment of China to GATT rules and disciplines and its earliest possible entry into GATT or its successor, the World Trade Organization (WTO). China's membership is crucial to effectively integrate China into the world economy and ensure the continuation of healthy market reforms in China. Of the two basic approaches to the China entry issue, we favor insisting that China make firm commitments to meet GATT/WTO standards. The value to the Trilateral countries of having China in the GATT/WTO is precisely to secure its adherence to GATT principles and disciplines, and this will be of great benefit to the Chinese economy as well.

2. Build on APEC

The Trilateral nations should build on the integrative mechanisms of APEC to foster further integration at the regional level. The dynamism and increasing interdependence of the Asia-Pacific region make APEC the natural venue for furthering China's economic integration. The participating economies of APEC should build on such agreements as the November 1993 Trade and Investment Framework, which, although non-binding, greatly contribute to regional economic liberalization. APEC should be used as a building-block for global economic integration. The compromise on membership worked out for the three parts of China can be relevant for larger multilateral trade groupings.

3. Loose Linkage between Economic Ties and Political Reform

We believe a loose linkage between political reform and expanded economic ties with Trilateral countries is appropriate, since these political reforms would contribute to China's long-run stability and attractiveness as an economic partner, as well as affect its human rights record. With regard to renewal of MFN status in the United States, we recommend a one-year renewal in expectation that China will continue to make progress in its adherence to internationally accepted basic human rights. Over time we hope the United States will be able to extend MFN treatment to China without an annual review.

4. Engage in Long-Term Investment

The Trilateral nations must be careful to work with China in building more sustainable, long-term economic growth, rather than exploiting a short-term boom. Ensuring that China will continue to grow and prosper is in everyone's interest. To that goal, the Trilateral nations should help China build institutions and regulatory mechanisms that will secure the future of market reforms and economic liberalization.

ESTABLISHING A NEW SECURITY ENVIRONMENT

The overarching goal in adapting to a new China in the security sphere is to work towards engagement, not containment. The Trilateral nations should view China as a potentially fruitful security partner, rather than as an impending security threat. Multilateral cooperation here is crucial. Towards these goals, we recommend:

1. Greater Transparency

China's defense policies are currently among the murkiest in the world. China would greatly contribute to improving the regional and global security environment if she more clearly articulated her national security priorities. Publishing an annual "white paper" outlining her defense policy would be a significant step towards alleviating rising fears in the region.

2. Build on Regional and Sub-Regional Security Groups

New regional security organizations, such as the ASEAN Regional Forum, and sub-regional groupings, such as a potential Korean Non-Nuclear Zone Framework, could be very helpful in improving the regional security environment. The Trilateral nations should encourage the growth of these groups, and promote the gradual development of confidence-building measures (CBMs) to strengthen relations in the region.

3. Wise Men Group for South China Sea

In order to seek a successful resolution to the conflict in the South China Sea, non-claimant countries within ASEAN—i.e., Indonesia, Singapore and Thailand—should take the lead in mediation. The Trilateral nations should support the development of a wise men group consisting of representatives from these three countries to undertake this conciliation effort.

4. Focus on Non-Proliferation

The Trilateral nations must engage China in a constructive dialogue on curtailing trade in weapons of mass destruction. China should be encouraged to adhere to international laws intended to control proliferation, such as the Nuclear Non-Proliferation Treaty (NPT) and the Missile Technology Control Regime (MTCR). Likewise, Trilateral nations must make it clear that they are also under the purview of these laws, and are not trying to simply edge China out of the arms market.

Trilateral nations should recognize that inclusion of China in the setting of NPT and MTCR regulations would significantly increase the chances of Beijing adhering to the results.

5. Encourage Responsible Military Behavior

While China's military was long overdue for a renewal program, the rapid rise in the defense budget and the increase in arms exports is disturbing. Aside from dialogue with China discouraging development of force projection capabilities, the Trilateral nations should back up these calls with aid policies conditioned on responsible military behavior. Aid should take into account military activity and expenditures, among other criteria. After all, military expenditures reduce the sums available for economic development. There should be exploration of how foreign aid can be used to prod China's defense development in a positive direction.

6. Avoid Provocative Action Towards China

In encouraging China to abide by non-proliferation norms and establish a non-aggressive stance, Trilateral nations must avoid actions that China deems threatening. Most obviously, the Trilateral nations should avoid selling weapons to Taiwan which enhance its force projection capability. China sees such actions as aggressive, and uses them to justify weapons sales to other unstable regions.

7. Maintain the U.S.-Japan Security Treaty

The U.S.-Japan security treaty is critical to sustain a healthy security environment in the region. We call on the United States to maintain a significant security presence in the region. China should not be used as a wedge to weaken the U.S.-Japan relationship. We warn against any nation, including China, playing old games of *realpolitik,* old "three kingdoms" games. Such activities are sure to destabilize the region, possibly leading to more violence and the disruption of the rising prosperity the region has enjoyed for the past few decades.

8. Europe's Role

Active European countries can in many ways articulate the broader international interest to China more clearly than the United States or Japan, whose security involvements with China are more immediate. Europe's role would also be strengthened if European Union members spoke with a more unified voice. It is time to move forward in both senses, in the framework of the Common Foreign and Security Policy.

So far, Member States have adopted "divergent approaches based solely on practical expediency....China is having to contend with national stances instead of a Community stance, a situation which only adds to the difficulty of working out and implementing a Community policy."[1]

9. Build Military-to-Military Contacts

With the aim of establishing greater communication and trust between China and other military powers, the Trilateral nations should work to improve military-to-military contacts with China at all levels. There should be increased effort to include China in regional and global peacekeeping operations (PKOs), and there should be further exploration of the possibilities for joint military operations.

GLOBAL ISSUES

On global issues, international action must, by definition, be multilateral. On the issues discussed below, this multilateral action needs to be highly coordinated in order to be effective. It is especially imperative that, in working on these issues, China be made a partner in action rather than a recipient of orders. Successful cooperation between China and the Trilateral nations would not only be effective in solving some of the world's most pressing problems, but would also provide a constructive venue for building trust more generally between China and the other world powers. To these ends, we recommend the following:

1. Focus on Non-Proliferation

The proliferation of weapons of mass destruction is one of the greatest threats in the post-Cold War era, and China's active participation in the campaign against proliferation will be crucial. China should participate in the nuclear test ban. It will be very important to make clear that international laws and regulations apply to all nations equally, and that China is not being unfairly targeted for her arms trade activities.

2. Use Foreign Aid to Guide Behavior

The Trilateral nations should consider using foreign aid grants to encourage certain behavior and discourage other actions. There should be increased grants allocated for environmental clean-up projects, or the purchasing of environmentally friendly technology.

Likewise, the Trilateral nations should consider making some aid contingent on improved behavior in certain areas, such as environmental action and military expenditures. We do not endorse setting up hard and fast conditionality between behavior and aid, but rather some sort of loose linkage.

3. Promote Information/Government Exchanges

Bilateral and multilateral exchange programs focused on furthering China's understanding of certain technologies could greatly enhance China's willingness to cooperate in global agreements. In particular, inviting Chinese specialists to examine how Trilateral countries have dealt with certain intransigent problems of industrial waste and air pollution can greatly assist Chinese endeavors to improve their environmental practices. Furthermore, such exchanges can create advocates for change within the Chinese government. In particular, establishing exchanges through existing international organizations (such as the UN and the IAEA) will make Beijing more comfortable with multilateral action, and with these organizations. By drawing Chinese participants further into UN activities, the Trilateral nations can help create a new generation of Chinese leaders who hold a more internationalist perspective.

HONG KONG AND TAIWAN

Within the continued framework of a "one China policy," the Trilateral countries should accord Taiwan a status commensurate with its economic and political accomplishments. This means Taiwan's admission to GATT should not be held hostage to the negotiations with the PRC, but should proceed on its own merits. Trilateral countries have obligations to help ensure that the people of Taiwan continue to enjoy a peaceful and prosperous future under democratic rule.

The fate of Hong Kong after July 1, 1997, will remain of keen concern and interest to the Trilateral countries, which have good cause to expect China to adhere to its commitments concerning the governance of Hong Kong as a separate, genuinely autonomous area. After developing a common approach, the Trilateral countries should quietly inform Beijing that a failure to implement its commitments would severely damage its relations with the outside world.

GOOD GOVERNANCE

The Trilateral nations do have a legitimate concern that China establish a more open political system, to ensure a responsible and responsive government, complete with the rule of law and due process. There also needs to be a concerted effort on the part of the Trilateral nations to approach issues of human rights in China with greater sensitivity and respect towards China's own culture and values. We have several suggestions for pursuing these goals:

1. Multilateral as well as Bilateral Approaches

The Trilateral nations should work with China on these issues on both a multilateral and a bilateral level. Multilateral approaches, when vigorously pursued, stand the best chance of success. China does wish to gain international respect and stature. If the Trilateral nations as a whole make clear that China must behave as an advanced nation to be treated as an advanced nation, she may be willing to improve her behavior. The actions of the G-7 nations at the 1990 Houston summit provide an example of the efficacy of this approach. Other multilateral actions, such as linking foreign aid to progress on human rights standards, should also be considered.

2. Work through International and Non-Governmental Organizations

The Trilateral nations should continue to rely on the information gathered by IOs and NGOs, and encourage them to continue in their work. There is much that can be done to further political liberalization through these groups. The Trilateral nations should make clear that as a permanent member of the UN Security Council, explicitly committed to upholding UN principles, China's current patterns of governance leave much to be desired.

3. Participate in Institution-Building

Both through bilateral and multilateral agencies, the Trilateral countries should join Chinese efforts to improve institutions that promote good and effective governance: a legal system, an independent judiciary, police and military establishments under the rule of law, a free press, and more effective parliamentary bodies. Not only would cooperation in these areas facilitate Chinese cooperation with the Trilateral countries, but these institutions are necessary for the guarantee of basic human rights and elimination of the abuse of power.

4. Engage in Cultural and Educational Exchanges

The gap in understanding between China and the Trilateral countries remains great. The Trilateral countries should help reduce this gap by fostering Chinese studies in their universities, by nurturing the social sciences and humanities in Chinese universities, by encouraging the Chinese government to permit accurate reporting of developments in China by journalists from throughout the world, by expanding cultural exchanges, and by funding the training of Chinese in Trilateral countries and encouraging the Chinese government to provide conditions that would entice these Chinese to return home and contribute to the development of their country.

CONCLUDING REMARKS

Even if each of the above recommendations were carried out to the letter, there can be no guarantees made about China's future. Indeed, the temptation most to be avoided is slipping into the belief that anyone outside China could determine China's future. China is ancient, huge and always unpredictable. It has experienced immense success in the past decade, more than was ever expected. It has huge resources to draw upon, and already successfully established ties to the outside world. There is little talk of China returning to the past, a near impossibility. Yet, that does not mean that there is any certainty about the future.

The Trilateral nations should approach China now with cautious optimism, and a willingness to be ready for the unexpected. China has no qualms about breaking the academic orthodoxy meant to delineate its behavior. To clearly see China as it changes so quickly, the Trilateral nations will need pragmatism and realism, rather than formulas that quickly become outdated.

While recognizing that there is no certainty as to what China's future holds, the Trilateral nations should recognize that their actions do affect China. Because of both the increasing interdependence in the global economy and China's own sensitivity to international opinion, Trilateral action could play a critical role in China's calculations and ultimate actions. The Trilateral nations must be careful to coordinate among themselves and with China. Our calls for multilateral action signify the need to include China, rather than "ganging up" on her. By engaging China now, and working with her to direct her growth in a sustainable, peaceful direction, perhaps the Trilateral nations can avoid needing to contain her in the future.

NOTES

I. Introduction: A New Rising Power

1. See Annex IV, *World Economic Outlook May 1993* (Washington, DC: IMF, 1993), pp. 116-19.

2. See "Table 5. Commercial energy" in *World Development Report 1993* (Washington, DC: World Bank, 1993), pp. 246-47. A column in this table presents energy consumption per capita (in kilograms of oil equivalent) for 1991. At 602, China is well below any Trilateral country in per capita terms (Portugal is lowest at 1,584 and Canada highest at 9,390), but when multiplied by population, China's total consumption is higher than any Trilateral country except the United States. At 692,300 million kilograms of oil equivalent (602 times 1,150 million people in 1991), China is far above Japan at 440,448 million kilograms (3,552 times 124 million people in 1991).

II. China in Historical Perspective

1. John King Fairbank, *China: A New History* (Cambridge: Harvard University Press, 1992). See also Charles O. Hucker, *China's Imperial Past: An Introduction to Chinese History and Culture* (Stanford: Stanford University Press, 1975); and Jonathan D. Spence, *The Search for Modern China* (New York: Norton, 1990).

2. John King Fairbank, ed., *The Chinese World Order: Traditional China's Foreign Relations* (Cambridge: Harvard University Press, 1968).

3. William T. Rowe, *Hankow: Commerce and Society in a Chinese City 1796-1889* (Stanford: Stanford University Press, 1984); and William T. Rowe, *Hankow: Conflict and Community in a Chinese City 1796-1889* (Stanford: Stanford University Press, 1989).

4. This theme is especially well developed in Mark Mancall, *China at the Center: 300 Years of Foreign Policy* (New York: Free Press, 1984).

5. This section draws heavily on Albert Feuerwerker, *The Foreign Establishment in China in the Early Twentieth Century* (Ann Arbor: University of Michigan Center for Chinese Studies, 1976).

III. The Mainland Domestic Context

1. Merle Goldman, ed., with Timothy Cheek, *China's Intellectuals and the State: In Search of a New Relationship* (Cambridge: Harvard University Press, 1987).

2. G. William Skinner, "The Structure of Chinese History," *Journal of Asian Studies* 44:2 (February 1985), pp. 271-92.

3. Nicholas Lardy, *Foreign Trade and Economic Reform in China 1978-90* (Cambridge: Cambridge University Press, 1992).

4. Vaclav Smil, *China's Environmental Crisis: An Inquiry into the Limits of National Development* (Armonk, NY: M.E. Sharpe, 1993).

5. Elizabeth Jean Perry, *Shanghai on Strike: The Politics of Chinese Labor* (Stanford: Stanford University Press, 1993); and Elizabeth Jean Perry, ed., with Jeffrey Wasserstrom, *Popular Protest and Political Culture in Modern China: Learning from 1989* (Boulder: Westview, 1992).

6. Michael D. Swaine, "The Military and Political Succession in China: Leadership, Institutions, Beliefs," RAND Report R-4252-AF (Santa Monica: RAND Corporation, 1992).

7. Perry Link, *Evening Chats in Beijing: Probing China's Predicament* (New York: Norton, 1992); Joseph Fewsmith, *Dilemmas of Reform in China: Political Conflict and Economic Debate* (Armonk, NY: M.E. Sharpe, 1994); and Robert C. Hsu, *Economic Theories in China, 1979-88* (Cambridge: Cambridge University Press, 1991).

IV. Hong Kong, Taiwan, and "Greater China"

1. Harry Harding, "The Concept of 'Greater China': Themes, Variations and Reservations," *China Quarterly* 136 (December 1993), pp. 660-86; and David Michael Lampton, "The Emergence of 'Greater China'," *China Quarterly* 136 (December 1993), pp. 653-59.

2. Tu Wei-ming, "Cultural China: The Periphery at the Center," *Daedalus* 120:2 (Spring 1991), pp. 1-32; and Tu Wei-ming, "Cultural Perspectives," *Daedalus* 122:2 (Spring 1993), pp. vii-xxiii.

3. Murray Weidenbaum, "Greater China: A New Economic Colossus?," *The Washington Quarterly* (Autumn 1993), p. 3.

4. The numbers in this paragraph are largely from the Office for China, Hong Kong and Mongolia at the U.S. Department of Commerce, unless otherwise noted.

5. S. Gordon Redding, *The Spirit of Chinese Capitalism* (Berlin: Walter de Gruyter, 1993).

6. Simon Holberton, "Hong Kong/Taiwan: Challenges Ahead," *Financial Times*, 18 November 1993, p. 8.

7. Ibid.

8. Barber B. Conable, Jr., and David M. Lampton, "China: The Coming Power," *Foreign Affairs* 71:5 (Winter 1992/93), p. 140.

9. Ibid., p. 139.

V. The Chinese Economy: Global and Regional Dimensions

1.   Nicholas R. Lardy, *China in the World Economy* (Washington: Institute for International Economics, 1994). The authors have relied on the Lardy book for a number of points in this chapter.

2.   Roderick MacFarquhar, ed., *The Politics of China 1949-1989* (Cambridge: Cambridge University Press, 1992).

3.   Harry Harding, *China's Second Revolution* (Washington, DC: Brookings Institution, 1987); Susan Shirk, *The Political Logic of Economic Reform in China* (Berkeley: University of California Press, 1993); and Michel Oksenberg with Bruce Dickson, "The Origins, Processes and Outcomes of Great Political Reform: A Framework of Analysis," in Dankwart A. Rustow and Kenneth Paul Erickson, eds., *Comparative Political Dynamics: Global Research Perspectives* (New York: Harper Collins, 1991).

4.   Tony Walker, "Long Leash for a Runaway Economy," *Financial Times,* 2 February 1994, p. 19.

5.   Daniel Southerland, "Western Firms Accuse China of Gouging Foreigners," *Washington Post,* 8 February 1994, p. A12.

6.   The European Union has been refused observer status in APEC. Some participation by observers from outside the Asia Pacific, perhaps from global economic organizations, might help reassure the rest of the world that APEC's intention to support global liberalization is being consistently pursued.

VI. China's National Security

1.   Fereidun Fesharaki, "Asia's Thirst for Middle East Oil" (Paper presented at the 2nd Middle East Petroleum and Gas Conference, 16-18 January 1994), p. 5.

2.   "China Protests US Trade Sanctions," *New York Times,* 28 August 1993. The comment was made by Deputy Foreign Minister Liu Huaqiu to the U.S. Ambassador, J. Stapleton Roy.

VII. Global Issues and China's Role

1.   "Biodiversity Treaty to Take Effect Dec. 29, UNEP Executive Director Says," *BNA Daily Report for Executives,* 5 October 1993, p. A191.

2.   "China, World Bank Sign Agreement to Phase Out Ozone Depleters," *Ozone Depletion Network Online Today,* 2 December 1993; and Bronwen Maddox and Tony Walker, "UK and China join ban on dumping nuclear waste at sea," *Financial Times,* 19 February 1994, p. 1.

3.   "Producers, Consumers of Tropical Woods Reach New International Accord on Trade," *BNA International Environment Daily,* 3 February 1994.

4. Michel Oksenberg, "China and the Japanese-American Alliance," in Gerald L. Curtis, ed., *The United States, Japan and Asia: Challenges for U.S. Policy* (New York: Norton, 1994, forthcoming).

5. Nicholas D. Kristof, "The Rise of China," *Foreign Affairs* 72:5 (November/December 1993), p. 66.

6. *World Development Report 1993* (Washington, DC: World Bank, 1993), pp. 90-91 and 216-19.

7. "China, Japan Agree to Sign Bilateral Environment Protection Treaty," *BNA International Environment Daily*, 20 December 1993.

8. Philip Boffey, "China and Global Warming," *New York Times*, 8 December 1993, p. A24.

9. "Pollution: It Will Get Worse," *Financial Times*, 18 November 1993, p. xi.

10. China is the only area still at 0.0 in the HIV line of two elaborate tables for 1990 in the World Bank's *World Development Report 1993* . See Tables B.2 and B.3 on pages 216 and 218.

11. In the World Bank's "worst case" scenario, by the year 2000, nearly four million more people each year would become infected with the AIDS virus in Asia as a whole. In the "optimistic case," new infections per year would still rise to well over one million per year, from about 250,000 in 1990. See page 101 of *World Development Report 1993.*

12. Ibid., p. 288.

13. Melissa Healy, "Clinton Unveils First Phase of Fast Action Global Warming Plan" *Los Angeles Times*, 20 October 1993, p. A5.

14. Anthony Rowley, "Japan set to be world's largest aid donor for next five years," *Business Times*, 19 June 1993, p. 15.

15. "China CO_2 Report: Use Less Coal Fuel, Boost Plant Efficiency to Clean Air," *Utility Environment Report*, 21 January 1994, p. 11.

VIII. The Effective and Good Governance of China

1. Donald J. Munro, *The Concept of Man in Contemporary China* (Ann Arbor: University of Michigan Press, 1977).

2. William Theodore de Bary, *The Liberal Tradition in China* (Hong Kong: Chinese University Press, 1983).

3. A. Doak Barnett, *China's Far West* (Boulder: Westview Press, 1993), pp. 642-52. Dr. Barnett conducted a full interview with Bao Tong, which is described in this section.

4. Lena Sun, "China Says It May Allow Red Cross To Inspect Conditions In Its Prisons," *Washington Post*, 10 November 1993.

5. For more extensive discussions of Tibet, see *Tibet: Issues for Americans*, National Committee on U.S.-China Relations Policy Series No. 4 (New York: NCUSCR, April 1992); Joseph Fletcher, "Tibet," in John King

Fairbank, ed., with Denis Twitchett, *The Cambridge History of China* (Cambridge: Cambridge University Press, 1978), vol. 10, pp. 90-106; John F. Avedon, *In Exile from the Land of Snows* (London: Michael Joseph, 1984); and Melvyn Goldstein, *History of Modern Tibet 1913-1951: The Demise of the Lamaist State* (Berkeley: University of California Press, 1989).

IX. Summary of Policy Recommendations

1.   European Parliament Report on Relations between the EU and the PRC, 7 January 1994.